A Traveler's Diary
from
1835

Karen Dustman

For adventurers near and far;
long ago and yet to come.

First Edition

Copyright © 2021- Karen Dustman
All Rights Reserved

Printed in the United States

 Table of Contents

Chapter 1: New York 7

Chapter 2: Ohio 8

Chapter 3: Michigan 12

Chapter 4: Illinois 30

Chapter 5: Missouri 62

Chapter 6: Kentucky/Illinois 66

Chapter 7: Indiana/Kentucky........... 68

Chapter 8: Ohio 79

Chapter 9: (West) Virginia/Ohio 82

Chapter 10: Pennsylvania................ 96

Chapter 11: New Jersey/Pennsylvania..... 119

Chapter 12: New York 121

For Further Reading 126
Local Historical Societies/Museums 140

INTRODUCTION

I purchased this lovely hand-written diary in 1988 in an antique shop in Cambria, California. At the time, its penciled entries had already survived over 150 years. Now, another 30 years have gone by.

What fascinated me then, as now, is the adventure this diary represents. With great hope, this gentleman set out from New York on a tour of America's "West" – what we now know as the Midwest.

We aren't positive of the identity of the man who wrote these words. One tiny clue about our writer's identity comes from the diary itself: a brief mention of his rice crop, suggesting he might have been a Southerner. "If you have not sold my rice and there should be any appearance of the march laying claim, I wish you to dispose of it before they get a preemption," he wrote.

More likely, however, is that he actually hailed from New England. The diary both begins and ends in New York State, for one thing. And the antique dealer I bought the diary from said she'd found it in Tiverton, Rhode Island (south of Newport). An 1830s newspaper clipping tucked in the back pages of the diary similarly came from a Newport paper.

Notations at the end provide us a likely guess for the man's name. The beginnings of a promissory note are sketched out in the diary's final pages, a personal document hinting that the diary *might* have belonged to one Elijah Brown of New Hampshire.

It was June, 1835, when our narrator set out with his friends on this journey. As nearly as we can tell, this party of six included two ladies, the "Misses" (probably really *Mrs.*) Buckley and Sturgis; a Mr. Buckley and Mr. Sturgis (likely their husbands); and gent named Mr. Russell.

A Traveler's Diary from 1835

The group got only as far as Tecumseh, Michigan, however, before the two ladies and their husbands became ill or wearied of the journey, and decided to return home. Maybe these two couples were older and more-easily fatigued. Bad roads, poor fare, and awful accommodations might have proven too much for gently-bred city ladies. More likely, however, some food-borne illness struck; Mr. Sturgis was said to be "in vomiting condition."

Nevertheless, our intrepid writer and his remaining companion, Mr. Russell, ventured on. His goal in this journey, as he expresses mid-trip in a letter home, was to find land where he'd like to settle (likely in Illinois); or to return home, satisfied that at least he had made the trip.

As we follow in his footsteps in our imagination, we see both great opportunities and great tragedies unfolding. Extensive canal systems and massive engineering feats like the Portage Railroad have just been completed, linking tiny, remote towns with the more-settled urban centers. Chicago is bustling with speculators, and land prices nearby are skyrocketing. But on the other hand, the Potawatomi and other Native Americans are losing both their land and their way of life, and soon will be forced to relocate away from everything that's been familiar.

I've corrected spellings and added punctuation for clarity, though I've done my best to keep the words and meaning intact. And as you'll see, I've fleshed out the often-brief descriptions with annotations and illustrations for context.

It's been a labor of love for me to figure out the details of this 1835 adventure from our diarist's brief and often cryptic notes. Filling in the backstory has given me the sort of education you never get in school.

This was real life, just as it was lived: the good, the bad, the sun, and the mud. Enjoy this 1835 journey!

A TRAVELER'S DIARY

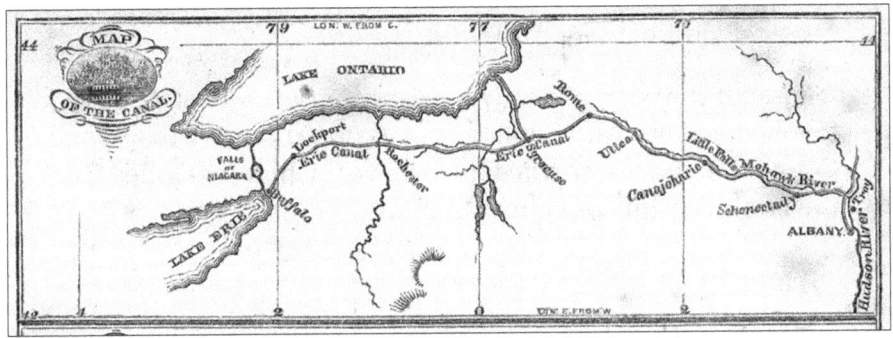

Map of the Erie Canal, showing Buffalo at left, beside Lake Erie. (1852 Jacob Abbott map, Library of Congress).

BUFFALO, NEW YORK
1835

June 1:

Arrived [at Buffalo] by way of the Canal at five this morning.

Breakfasted at the *City Hotel*, kept by Allen in miserable style.

      Food paid for Breakfast: .37-1/2
      Boots & Baggage to Steam Boat .12-1/2

> **HOTELS.**
> There are a great number of Hotels in the City, which the great influx of travellers renders necessary. Among the most noted of which are the American Hotel, Eagle Tavern, Mansion House, Farmer's Hotel, and City Hotel. There are several others which are kept, and conducted in a style not surpassed by any others in the western country.

Although our traveler found the City Hotel's breakfast fare lacking, this was one of the "most noted" hotels in town, according to the 1836 Buffalo City Directory.

A Traveler's Diary from 1835

Took passage at nine [a.m.] on board Steam Boat *Michigan* for Detroit. The *Michigan* is one of the best Boats on the Lake.

Paid Boat fare to Detroit: $8.00.

Passed Dunkirk at twelve, passed Erie at five; 8 o'clock touched at Connyat [*Conneaut, Ashtabula County*] for wood. Connyat is in [*the northeast corner of*] Ohio, two miles from the boundary line of Pennsylvania.

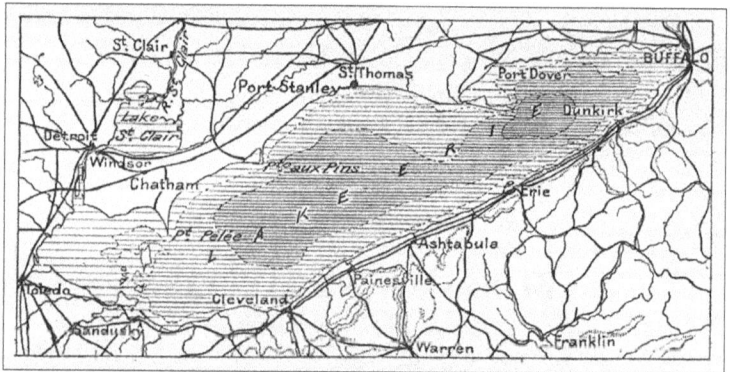

An 1885 map showing Buffalo (top right); Erie; and Ashtabula (where Conneaut is located) along the southern shore of Lake Erie.

Our traveler was an early passenger on the newly-completed Erie Canal, which had been finished just ten years earlier (1825). At 363 miles in length, the Canal was considered a major engineering feat – over twice the length of canals found in Europe.

Promoters had claimed that the Erie Canal would "bind the nation," tying the well-settled Eastern region with the largely untouched interior. And indeed it did. Later historians would emphasize the canal's important role in facilitating settlement of the Midwest. The growing influx of white settlers also would accelerate displacement of the Native Americans who'd long called the interior regions home.

Buffalo was something of a dead-end for the Erie Canal in 1835, leading to congestion at the terminus of the canal. Although a con-

tract was let in 1831 for construction of one smaller "slip" or side-canal connecting the Canal directly with Lake Erie, a helpful network of additional slips would not be completed until the 1840s.

Our passenger booked steamboat passage to carry him on Lake Erie from Buffalo to Detroit, a hefty $8.00 expense. This was the "cabin fare"; steerage would have been just $3.00.

After leaving Buffalo, it was no coincidence that our traveler's steamboat stopped at Conneaut, Ohio to take on wood. Conneaut Creek emptied into Lake Erie here on the southern shore, creating a good natural harbor, and the town was a regular stop for steamboats.

The first survey of the Conneaut area had been made in 1796, with European settlers beginning a permanent settlement in 1798. When our traveler arrived, the area was still in its infancy. Conneaut Village had only been incorporated in 1834, the year prior to his arrival. A second survey would soon be made in 1837.

An 1878 sketch of the residence of Thomas Gibson, one of the earliest settlers at Conneaut, Ohio, who'd arrived in the township in 1830.

A Traveler's Diary from 1835

The Steamer Michigan, commanded by Capt. Chesley Blake, amid a gale. (Maritime History of the Great Lakes).

June 2:

Touched at five in the morning at Fairport [*Harbor*] for wood, situated at the mouth of Grand River.

At eight, touched and remained one hour at Cleveland, [*Ohio*]. Spent the time in viewing the place, was much pleased with it. It is high and pleasantly located, business apparently good and improvements extending on both sides of the River.

Sketch of Superior Street in Cleveland, west of the Public Square, made by T. Whepley in 1833. (Library of Congress).

A Traveler's Diary from 1835

> **FIRST TRIP THIS SEASON OF THE STEAMBOAT**
> **MICHIGAN,**
> *TO THE UPPER LAKES.*
>
> THE Steamboat MICHIGAN, Captain C. BLAKE, will leave Buffalo on Friday the 19th of June next, at 9 o'clock, A. M. for Lake Michigan. The following are the ports at which she will touch during the voyage, after leaving Detroit, viz:
>
> Mackinac, Green Bay, Milwalkie, Chicago, Mighigan City, New Buffalo, St. Joseph, and Grand River,. She will also touch at the intermediate ports on Lake Erie, up and down.
>
> The *MICHIGAN* has two low pressure engines of great power, and her accommodations are equal in extent and elegance to any boat now afloat. She was built principally for the upper trade, and her commander is a gentleman of experience and skill in the navigation of the western lakes. By this boat, passengers will have an opportunity of viewing all the prominent points of interest on Lakes Huron and Michigan—and will return to Buffalo, in from fifteen to seventeen days. For berths or state rooms, apply to
>
>   OLIVER NEWBERRY, *Detroit.*
>   BARKER & HOLT, *Buffalo.*
> Buffalo, May 27, 1835.   4t sw 6

Our traveler may have found his berth aboard the Steamboat Michigan by answering an ad similar to this one in Buffalo's Democratic Free Press of June 17, 1835.

Twelve, passed a river cutter. Half past one, touched at Huron to land and receive passengers. Half past five, passed the Sisters; between those Islands Perry gained his victory 10th September 1814.

At seven, passed [Fort] Malden, beautifully situated on the Canada shore, but badly improved.

Ten [*p.m.*], landed at Detroit. The fare and accomodations on board of the *Michigan* were very superior. Her tonnage about 500. Commanded by Capt. Blake, who is very rough and rather ungentlemanly in his manners, but apparently perfectly competent and master of his business.

Took lodgings at the *Steam Boat Hotel*, a House badly managed, full of dirt and filth. The best and only place we could get in.

Found the Stages all engaged for two days ahead. Secured seats for the Friday morning's Stage.

Paid Stage fare to Niles – 9.50.

Cleveland was growing rapidly in 1835 when our traveler and his companions paid it a flying one-hour visit. The city's population would jump from just over a thousand souls in 1830 to 6,071 in 1840 (catapulting it to 45th in size in the nation). The year after our traveler arrived, the City of Cleveland would receive its city charter.

The "Sisters" he mentions passing are three islands, part of a group of islands at the head of Lake Erie. As he indicates, Naval Officer Oliver Hazard Perry won a famous victory over the British Navy here on September 10, 1813 during the "Battle of Lake Erie" in the War of 1812 (although our writer incorrectly gives the year of the battle as 1814). Perry's Victory & International Peace Memorial is now located on a South Bass Island, Ohio, another of these islands.

The steamboat Michigan, which our traveler found "very superior," was 472.43 tons and was captained by Capt. Chesley (or Chelsea) Blake. A tall man said to be almost a "giant" in stature,

Capt. Blake had fought in the War of 1812 and by the time our traveler met him, had become a "titan of Great Lakes shipping." But just as our traveler noted, Capt. Blake was well-known for his salty language. A contemporary would later reminisce: "Unlike most of the lake captains of those days, who were perfect gentlemen in manners and dress, he affected none of these: no courtly phrases, no ruffled shirt, no blue coat with brass buttons... his use or abuse of the King's English was somewhat phenomenal."

After Capt. Blake died of cholera in 1849, a mourner paid homage to his kind heart: "Rough as the billows whose impotent assaults on his vessel he ever laughed to scorn; with voice as hoarse as the tempest which he delighted to rule, this gallant son of the sea had withal a woman's tenderness of heart to answer the appeals of distress."

The Steamer Michigan continued on to Chicago after dropping our traveler at Detroit. As luck would have it, a copy of her manifest on that subsequent voyage has survived: see https://images.maritimehistoryofthegreatlakes.ca/110336/data.

After reaching Detroit, our traveler did not much care for the Steamboat Hotel, located at the corner of Woodbridge and Randolph Streets. He wasn't alone in his dissatisfaction; it had other unhappy customers as well. Amos Andrew Parker, a visitor from New Hampshire, described the dinnertime melee:

> "When the bell rang for dinner, . . . [a]ll in and about the house jumped and run as if the house had been on fire, and I thought that to have been the case. I followed the multitude, and found they were only going into the hall to dinner. It was a rough and tumble game at knife and fork — and whoever got seated first, and obtained the best portion of dinner, was the best fellow. Those who came after must take care of themselves the best way they could; and were not always able to obtain a very abundant supply."

Parker also complained about the hotel's poor accommodations: "At night, I was obliged to sleep in a small room having three beds in it, take a companion, and a dirty bed." Little wonder our traveler was unimpressed with the lodgings. The Steamboat Hotel would succumb to a fire in 1837.

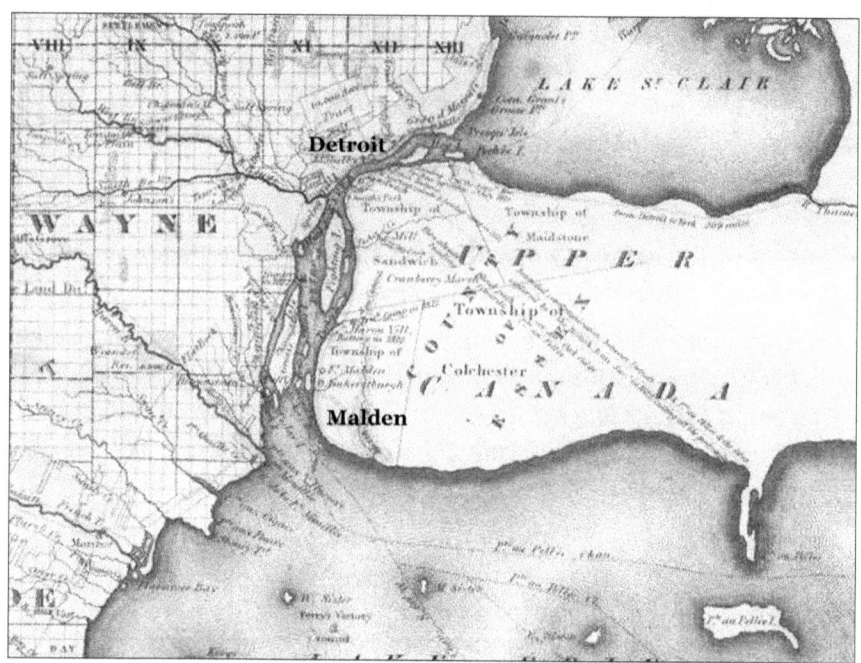

Malden is located near the confluence of the Detroit River and Lake Erie, on the Canadian (eastern) side of the river. Detroit is on the west side just above "Fighting Island," near Lake St. Clair. (1826 map by John Farmer, Library of Congress).

A Traveler's Diary from 1835

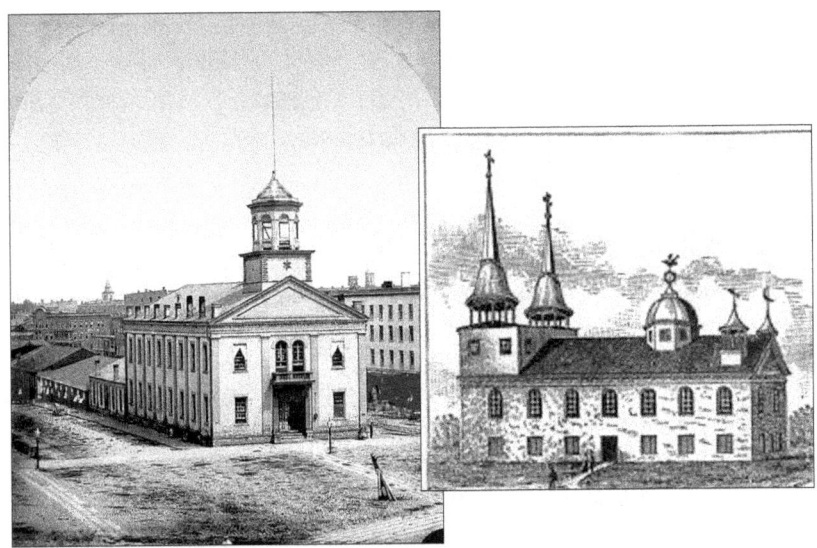

Two of the Detroit buildings our traveler may have spotted during his visit: City Hall (left), built in 1835; and St. Anne's Catholic Church (right), whose cornerstone had been laid in 1818 at the corner of Larned and Bates Streets.

June 3:

Took a very inferior Breakfast. I walked out to view the place [*Detroit, Michigan*], found the business part filthy dirty.

The upper part, where the most genteel inhabitants reside, is very pleasant and has some fine dwellings with many pretty gardens.

Afternoon, crossed the Ferry to Richmond on the Canada side. It is finely situated. The inhabitants are mostly French and apparently have no idea of ever making the place better by improvements. Enterprise would make it a beautiful place.

Paid for washing & [*cleaning*] 2 [*pair*] boots - .50

The "business" section of Detroit visited by our traveler was likely West Jefferson, at the southern end of today's Financial District, and nearby Griswold Street. Some historians peg 1831 as the birth of the Financial District, when the Bank of Michigan moved to Jefferson near Woodward. Our traveler may well have passed this bank on his walk, and perhaps also the Farmers' & Mechanics' Bank, built in 1832 on Jefferson near Griswold.

Nearby, as our traveler noted, was an upper-class residential district, which would eventually be absorbed by the Financial District as it grew. Judge McDonnell's residence in the 1830s, for example, was at the northwest corner of Fort and Shelby Streets.

What our traveler called 'Richmond' on the Canadian side was likely really the town of Windsor, Ontario, a small French settlement established in 1749. (There's a 'Sandwich' neighborhood on Windsor's west side, so perhaps our traveler confused "wich" and "rich".) Only 300 people would live in Windsor as late as 1846, so the population was likely even smaller in 1835, when our diarist paid his visit by ferry.

1881 map showing the Canadian town of Windsor and the Sandwich neighborhood, directly across the river from Detroit. (Wikipedia).

A Traveler's Diary from 1835

Young Stevens Mason, just 23 years old, was elected Michigan's first governor in October, 1835, during the same election that approved the proposed state constitution.

June 4:

Visited Convention which meets here [*Detroit*] for forming Constitution for the State.

    Paid board, Steam Boat Hotel – 2.25

Detroit had been incorporated as a city in 1815. But Michigan was still only a territory, not yet a state, when our traveler paid his visit in 1835.

The state's constitutional Convention mentioned by our traveler was held at the Territorial Capitol in Detroit (the Territorial Courthouse, built in 1828). Sessions of this Convention would last three more weeks, until June 24, 1835, when the 91 delegates approved the draft constitution.

Michigan voters would approve that proposed constitution a few months later, on October 5, 1835. But the U.S. Congress refused to officially admit Michigan as a state until a boundary dispute with next-door Ohio was resolved. The disputed strip of land at Michigan's southern border included the important port city of Toledo. The property in dispute was known as the 'Toledo Strip.'

The Territorial Courthouse in Detroit, built in 1824, is where delegates met in 1835 for the state's Constitutional Convention, and where our diarist paid a visit to hear the proceedings. The central tower is similar to that of Detroit's City Hall, built in 1835 (see previous pages).

Matters grew heated. Competing laws were passed, and state militias were called up. The thorny boundary dispute festered on for another full year, until Gov. Mason finally agreed to cede the disputed strip of land to Ohio, gaining in exchange the western two-thirds of the Upper Peninsula for Michigan. Not everyone liked this solution, however. And according to some scholars, there may have been a bit of political funny business in the December, 1836 Convention in Ann Arbor, during which Mason's hand-picked delegates finally approved the compromise.

Michigan finally was admitted as the 26th state in the Union on January 26, 1837.

A Traveler's Diary from 1835

Humorous illustration of a stagecoach ride by J. Ross Browne, 1861.

June 5 (Friday):

Five in the morning, took [*the*] Stage for Niles, [*Michigan*]. Breakfasted eight miles from Detroit.

Traveled all day on a most horrid Road – this section is low and unhealthy.

Reached Ypsilantia [*Ypsilanti*], 32 miles from Detroit, and dined at half past five.

    Dinner & Breakfast - .75

Continued on all night. Road growing worse all the time. Part of the time had to go on foot, nearly knee-deep in mud.

Ypsilanti is west of Detroit, on the west bank of the Huron River. The spot was originally a Native American river crossing and camp site. In 1809, three French explorers built a trading post there. And in 1825, three local settlers laid out a townsite plat. It was named for a contemporary Greek freedom-fighter who'd successfully held off the Turkish army with his small forces, despite being greatly outnumbered.

An initial survey was done in 1825 for a new road that would connect Detroit with Chicago, known (of course) as the "Chicago Road." It started as a military effort to connect the forts at both ends. But settlers and travelers soon eagerly made use of it as well.

Commercial stagecoach service was already available from Detroit to Ypsilanti by 1830. By the end of 1835, when the Chi-

Road Contracts.

CONTRACTS for constructing the road leading from Detroit to Chicago, commencing at the 136th mile stake, and from thence to the Indiana line, including the sections heretofore let, will be offered at public auction, and sold to the lowest bidder, at the house of Mr. Sherwood, Edwardsburgh, on Thursday the 4th of June next. The road, except which passes over low ground, will be constructed in the following manner, to wit: To be opened 100 feet wide; of which 80 feet are to be grubbed, the grubholes filled, and the ground make level and cleared of timber, stones, brush &c; 21 feet on each side, to be low chopped, and the remainder to be chopped to suit the contractor. Contracts for the bridges over Crooked and Christain creeks will be let; and if there are sufficient funds, for that over the St. Joseph River, will also be entered on the day of sale. The usual security for the performance of the contracts will be required. Five per cent per month will be deducted for every month which shall elapse, between the 20th of December next (when the contracts are to be completed) and their actual completion.

E. S. SIBLEY, Lieut. on Eng. Duty.
Detroit, May 5, 1835.   3w2

The publisher of the White Pigeon Statesman is requested to insert the above till sale, and forward his bill to this office.

Democratic Free Press, May 6, 1835.

cago Road was finished, the Western Stage Company had two stages leaving Detroit every day, with the entire journey to Chicago taking four and a half days.

But when our traveler made his journey, bids had just closed for work on the new Chicago Road, so the road wasn't yet complete.

The early roadway our traveler followed wasn't in great condition, as he noted in his diary. Even when the entire Chicago Road was eventually finished later that same year, much of it was "little

A Traveler's Diary from 1835

more than an unimproved trail," as one later historian would say, "making a trip over it an unforgettable and an uncomfortable experience." That certainly seemed to be the case for our traveler!

If our diarist had waited another three years, he would have found his journey far easier. A railroad line connected Detroit with Ypsilanti in 1838.

STAGES.

TERRITORIAL ROAD, (Western Route.)

For Ann Arbor, Jacksonburgh, Marshall, Kalamazoo, and St. Joseph,—the mail stage leaves sundays, Tuesdays, Thursdays and Saturdays, at 12 o'clock, M. and the accommodation stage on Mondays, Wednesdays, and Fridays, at 5 o'clock, P M
Office, Corner of Jefferson & Woodward Avenues.

EASTERN ROUTE,

For Buffalo via Monroe, Manhattan, Toledo, Maumee City, Perrysburgh, & Sandusky—a mail stage leaves every morning at 5 o'clock:
Office, Corner of Jefferson & Woodward Avenues.

WESTERN ROUTE,

For Chicago via Ypsilanti, Saline, Clinton, Tecumseh, Jonesville, Coldwater, White Pigeon, Niles, Michigan City, &c—a stage leaves on Mondays, Wednesdays, Fridays, at 5 o'clock in the morning, and on Sundays Tuesdays, Thursdays and Saturdays at 12 o'clock, M

BOARDMAN & SALTMARSH,
GILLIS & HUGHES,
JONES & BROWNE,
ROBERT FORSYTHE,
} *Proprietors.*

Office, Corner Jefferson & Woodward Avenues.

DETROIT.

WESTERN STAGE CO.

Office, Woodward Avenue,
Corner of Jefferson Avenue.

Three daily Lines of Stages leave the office of the Western Stage company;—one via Ypsilanti, Tecumseh Jonesville, White Pigeon, Niles, Michigan City to Chicago, through in four and a half days—one via Plymouth, Ann Arbor, Jacksonburgh, and Marshall to Kalmazoo, through in two days and a half—one via Monroe Toledo, Perrysburgh to Lower Sandusky, through in two days. Extras furnished on all of the above roads at the shortest notice.
JAMES L. GILLIS
Treasurer of the Western Stage Co.

A partial listing of stages in the Detroit City Directory for 1837. (Two additional stage lines, identified on a subsequent directory page, served Flint River and Ft. Gratiot.)

Our traveler evidently took the 5 a.m. stage by Western Stage Co. for his journey to Ypsilanti and beyond.

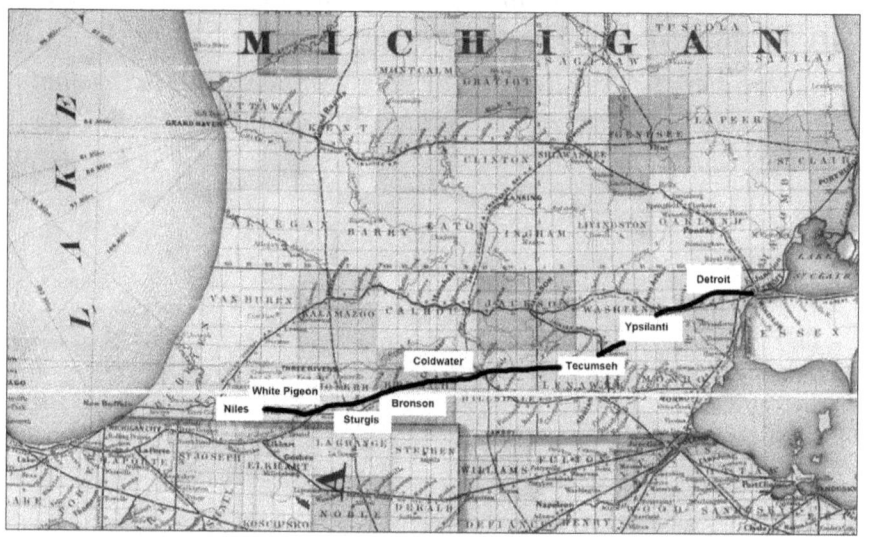

1859 map by G.W. Colton (Library of Congress), annotated to show our traveler's route across southern Michigan as he headed west from Detroit.

June 6 and 7:

Arrived at Tecumseh, [*Michigan*] at five in the morning. Took breakfast and continued on, leaving Miss Sturgis sick. [*The*] Buckleys, on account of the fatigue of traveling, [*also*] could not go on.

    Paid for meals as we found them on the Road – $1.50.

One o'clock, passed the head waters of the North Branch of Raisin River – rolling land and healthy country.

Two o'clock [*p.m.*], arrived at Coldwater, got a bed for the first time since leaving Detroit.

[*We were*] called at five [*a.m.* June 7]. Breakfasted and proceeded on.

    Paid Breakfast and for Lodgings – .38

A Traveler's Diary from 1835

Coldwater would grow rapidly in the next thirty years. This sketch from 1868 shows a sizeable town. (A. Ruger "Birds Eye View of Coldwater," Library of Congress).

The town of Coldwater is situated on Coldwater River, which empties into St. Joseph's River, and is navigable for boats *etc.*, say 3 feet of water.

Left Coldwater at seven [*a.m.*]. Plenty of good lands can be taken in this vicinity at Government prices. This country, from appearances, is unquestionably healthy.

9 [*a.m.*], stopped and watered our horses at Freedom Hotel in Branch County, seven miles [*west*] from Coldwater. Land does not appear as good as in Hillsdale County.

Half past nine, passed Prairie River; ten [*a.m.*], Bronson's Prairie in St. Joseph's County. In this county the lands are said to be equal to any in Michigan – but it is not the case.

Twelve [*noon*], arrived at French's Inn [*on foot*] in advance of the Stage, the horses having failed or mired down. Dined at one.

    Paid dinner – .38

At four [*p.m.*], crossed Sturgis's Prairie, about five thousand acres of beautiful land surrounded by fine timber. The Prairie is all under fine cultivation, valued at ten dollars per acre.

Half past five, passed Klinger's Lake, 8 miles from White Pigeon Prairie. In this vicinity, the land is very fine, what are termed 'Burr openings' and denotes the very best quality. It is rolling [*country*], thickly covered with Burr Oaks interspersed with fine, large timber, far superior to anything I ever saw, and the only part of Michigan I have been pleased with; healthy and good water.

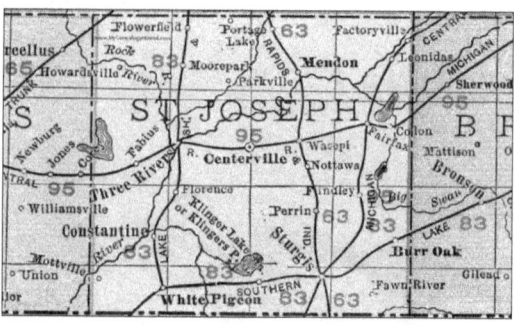

This 1911 map of St. Joseph County shows Sturgis, Klinger Lake, and White Pigeon, toward the bottom of the map.

Seven [*p.m.*], arrived at Pigeon Prairie [*White Pigeon*].

Paid for tea – .38

Traveled all night.

The stage route that our traveler bumped along from Detroit to Chicago followed the Old Sauk Trail. This was an ancient game and trading trail used for centuries by multiple Native American tribes, including the Sauk, Chippewa, and Potawatomi. In later years, this same route was followed (more or less) by today's Highway 12.

Branch, Michigan was named for John Branch, Secretary of the Navy under President Andrew Jackson. A settler named Jabe Bronson had built a residence nearby in 1828, and another early settler named Hugh Campbell erected a log home in 1830. Branch County was organized in 1833; Coldwater would eventually become its county seat. So while Native Americans had lived and hunted here for centuries, white settlements were still new at the time our traveler visited in 1835.

By 1837, two years after our traveler's visit, Coldwater City had a population of 140 souls, and Coldwater Township was home to 960.

Some thirty years later, by 1868, Coldwater had become a sizeable town, as the sketch above shows.

Cholera epidemics had hit Detroit in 1832 and again in 1834, which may help explain our traveler's concern with the healthfulness of his surroundings. Although our traveler pronounced the Coldwater area 'unquestionably healthy,' an outbreak of malaria would strike the town just two years later, in 1837.

'Burr openings' refers to the open habitat favored by Burr Oak trees, which typically are found in an oak savanna, rather than a densely-packed forest.

Chief Crane of the Potawatomi Tribe with a fellow tribal member, circa 1855. (Library of Congress, Brady-Handy Collection).

June 8:

Half past five, stopped at Adams Port [*today's Adamsville, Michigan*], 15 miles from Niles. Breakfasted at Edwardsburg in Bardsley Prairie, [*Michigan*]. In this vicinity there are good lands at Government prices.

Paid Breakfast - .37

Half past ten, arrived at Niles. Abandoned the Stage.

Niles is situated on the River St. Joseph, fifty miles from Lake Michigan; has eight hundred inhabitants, water very good. Town lots $1 to $12.00 dollars. Appears to be increasing.

Two decades after our traveler visited, Niles would be a prosperous place indeed. View of the Arcade Block in Niles (inset from 1860 map, Library of Congress).

Visited the Indian preserves. Very excellent soil, mostly taken up, with expectations of holding it by prescription right when it comes in to market. The Indian settlement is about four miles from Niles on the opposite side of St. Joseph's River. The Indian reserve lands contain one hundred sections, [*each*] ten miles square, or 100 square miles. It is supposed those lands can not come in to market short of eighteen months, in consequence of the stipulated time for the Indians to remain if they wish.

A flour mill at Niles (inset from 1860 map, Library of Congress).

Niles has many advantages and no doubt could be made a place of considerable importance if it should fall in the hands of enterprising men with a moderate capital.

It has in the vicinity several mills, flouring and sawing, mostly situated on a fine stream called the Dowagiac and empties into the St. Joseph one mile below Niles. The River St. Joseph could be dammed at small expense and the water used to good advantage. It is supposed it will be done. The population has doubled in ten months.

There are lands within a few miles of this place of the best quality that are not entered, and it is said some are not more than one mile from the St. Joseph River, which I think worthy of attention.

This is one of the first entries suggesting our traveler's primary purpose for his lengthy journey: scouting for land to buy and a suitable place to relocate.

Today's Adamsville, Michigan, founded in 1832, was originally known as Adamsport, as our traveler called it. Just three years after our traveler's visit, it would merge (in 1838) with Sage's Mill across the creek.

For white settlers, this was a time of rapid expansion and new beginnings. For Native Americans, it was a time of great tragedy. The Potawatomi People were being separated from their ancestral lands in Michigan and moved to reservations pursuant to multiple treaties, including the 1829 Treaty of Prairie du Chien and the 1833 Treaty of Chicago. The promise was that the United States would provide food, supplies, and funding to help tribal members establish new homes.

In 1838, many of the Potawatomi in Michigan were forced to move west, an event that has been called the 'Potawatomi Trail of Death.' Leopold Pokagon and his villagers, however, were able to purchase land in Silver Creek Township and remained in Michigan. Roughly 150 years later, on September 21, 1994, the Pokagon Band of Potawatomi was formally recognized by the federal government as a tribe, reaffirming their sovereignty.

A Traveler's Diary from 1835

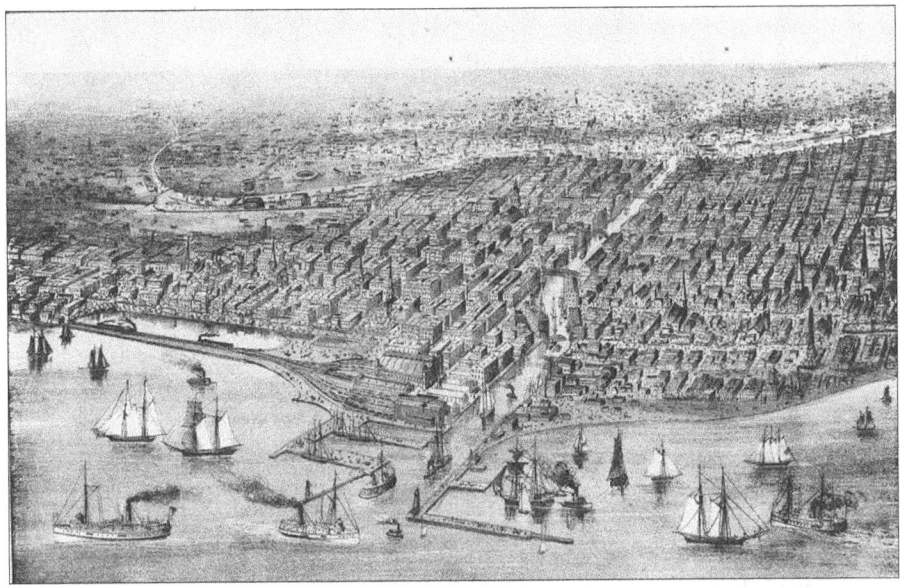

Chicago "As It Was" (Currier & Ives litho, circa 1856, Library of Congress).

June 9:

Spent at Niles, [Michigan].

June 10:

Paid [steamboat] fare at Niles. Took Steamboat *David Crockett* at eight [a.m.] for mouth of [the] St. Joseph.

At nine, on the border of the River, saw Cousin, war chief of the Potawatomi tribe. Stopped on the river five miles from Niles for wood.

The steamboat *David Crockett* cost $800 complete, an article not to be described. The stream, St. Joseph River, runs down at the rate of 4 miles an hour.

[At] 3 o'clock, arrived at St. Joseph's, situated on Lake Michigan. The town [is] about ten houses, situated on a high sand Bluff. Requires some improvements, which are about to be made, to make a good harbor. The opposite bluff has been purchased at a great price by a company of individuals on speculation.

Took [a] packet, crossed the Lake [Michigan], arrived at Chicago, [Illinois] next morning.

A "Buffalo & Chicago" steam packet called the Empire State (1835 Library of Congress).

Here [at Chicago] everything is bustle and confusion. A very hard place to get to, and harder to get away. The stages are engaged for a week to ten days ahead, impossible to get into a decent House. [The] rage of speculation here amounts almost to gambling. Land that was not considered worth five dollars an acre here three years ago would now sell for as many hundred thousand dollars [$500,000].

Paid Inn at St. Joseph - .38

Packet fare to Chicago – 3.00

The steamboat David Crockett would sink just a year later, on August 1, 1836, after hitting a rock between Niles and St. Joseph.

☞ The Constantine Republican of the 17th says that the Steamboat David Crockett which has been running on the St. Joseph's River for the last two years, was lately sunk between Niles and St. Joseph, by striking a rock while under headway.

Buffalo Daily Commercial Advertiser, August 25, 1836.

Ft. Dearborn as it looked in 1856, with blockhouse and lighthouse. (Rufus Blanchard lithograph, Library of Congress).

June 11:

Excitement and speculation exceeds everything I have ever witnessed.

Towns are laid out all along through where the canal will probably cross, cut into lots and sold at one time. I witnessed the sale of lots in the town of Dresden, 55 miles from this place [*Chicago*]. They sold from $40 to $140 [*and*] over; the excitement has been so great that strangers that knew nothing about it would purchase at these prices.

Visited Fort Dearborn, from which you have a most beautiful view of the Lake. The Government reserve is decidedly the pleasantest part of the place.

Paid Steam Boat Hotel - .75

Left at 4 [*a.m.*] in the best wagon and horses we could procure, which were poor enough. After leaving Chicago [*traveling southwest*], entered a large, wet prairie ten miles across, covered from six to 18 inches with water. Horses could not drag out of the walk.

Tedious way. To the end we arrived [*at*] Mrs. Barry's, the only house to be got at for the night; found it thronged. The floor for about forty of us was the best could be done for us.

That was considering [*that*] the night before, in crossing the Lake, we were tumbled to the number of one hundred in a small vessel's hold, there to sleep without bed or blanket – pretty hard fare.

The Steamboat Hotel where our traveler stayed in Chicago was located on North Water Street near Kinzie, and in 1835 was managed by John Davis. It would change hands the following year, and with William McCorristen at the helm, became the 'American Hotel.'

Illinois was undergoing rapid change at the time of our traveler's arrival. One historian estimates that as many as 1,000 new towns were platted during the boom of 1835-1837, and two million acres of land changed hand in 1835 alone.

Chicago itself had grown up around Ft. Dearborn, originally settled back in 1804. And Illinois had been admitted as a state as early as 1818. So what drove this sudden land frenzy in the mid-1830s?

Well, a sudden crush of settlers, for one thing. Between 1830 and 1835, Illinois' population doubled. It would nearly double again between 1835 and 1840.

Speculators thrived during this excitement. Some sellers of Chicago town lots boldly assured would-be investors that they could double their money in a few short months. Auctions for new town lots also helped drive the fever, sometimes with shills in the audience helping bid up prices.

There were also legitimate land deals to be had. If you didn't want to risk buying a town lot, agricultural land could be purchased at a *federal Land Office for $1.25 per acre (the "government prices" our traveler had mentioned earlier). But getting accurate information about "government land" also was difficult, as our traveler would later comment.*

The proposed town of Dresden was located between Chicago and St. Louis — though at the time its lots were being auctioned off, the road connecting those two towns had not yet been built. The sale of town lots which our traveler mentions likely did not take place at the future townsite itself but rather somewhere in Chicago. Dresden lots had similarly been sold the previous week (June 4) at the Missouri Hotel in St. Louis, with only a plat of the proposed townsite for bidders to examine.

But all good things must come to an end. The Illinois land frenzy would come to a screeching halt with the nation-wide financial panic of 1836-37. Prices dropped, at least until 1839.

Our traveler drops a mention here of a proposed canal. The success of the Erie Canal had inspired similar canal-building efforts elsewhere in the country, and connecting the Great Lakes with the Mississippi River had long been a dream for Illinois. In 1822, Congress authorized a canal joining the Chicago and Illinois Rivers, offering land grants to sweeten the deal. Initial funding for this effort failed, and in 1827, Congress authorized even more extensive land grants. But again, financial backing proved slim. Finally, in 1835, the State of Illinois authorized bonds to construct the canal, and in January, 1836, agreed to back those bonds with the state's own credit. And <u>that</u> assurance would finally get the canal project rolling.

Ground was broken at Chicago on July 4, 1836 for the Illinois & Michigan Canal, just a year after our traveler passed through. Work on the canal continued as late as 1841, but the state defaulted on its bond interests payments that July. More drama and difficulty followed before the 96-mile-long I&M Canal finally opened in April, 1848, successfully linking Chicago with La Salle.

Nearly a century later, in 1933, the Illinois Waterway would render the old I&M Canal obsolete. But this early canal route was designated a National Heritage Corridor in 1984.

Land Agents.

NORTH-WESTERN LAND AGENCY,
Chicago, Illinois.
Office on Kinzie Street, East of Dearborn.

OGDEN & JONES,
GENERAL LAND AGENTS,
FOR THE
NORTH-WESTERN STATES AND TERRITORIES.
WILLIAM B. OGDEN.   WILLIAM E. JONES.

J. B. F. RUSSELL
Has established an office for the transaction of
GENERAL LAND AGENCY,
AT
CHICAGO,
For the payment of taxes, purchase, or sale of Lands, Lots, &c. &c.

Land agent listings in the 1844 Chicago City Directory.

A Traveler's Diary from 1835

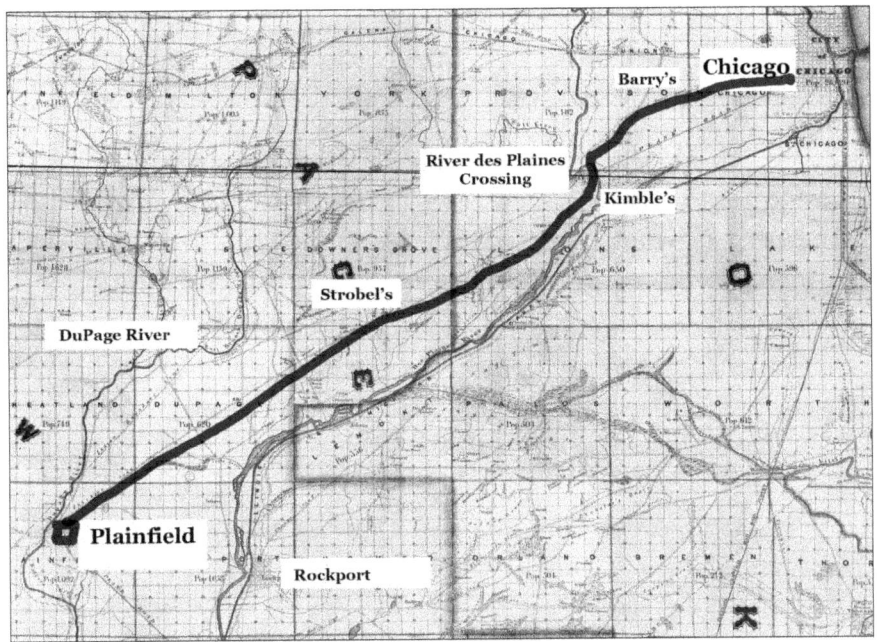

1851 map of Cook, DuPage and other Illinois counties, by James H. Rees, annotated to show our traveler's approximate route. (Library of Congress).

June 12:

Half past 4 [*a.m.*], paid Mrs. B[*arry*] - .37-1/2 and continued on [*southwest from Chicago*].

Forded River des Plaines, traveled through wet and low prairie, took breakfast at Kimble's - .25

Continued through a much better [*section*] of rolling prairie with some small groves of timber. Alternately rain and sunshine on the way, uncomfortable with no covering to protect [*us*].

Dined at Strobel's 30 miles from Chicago.

[*At*] four, our horses gave out; stopped at Plainfield Exchange, chartered another team to proceed in the morning.

The farm on which this House is situated [is] on the River du Page in the Town of Plainfield; 100 acres, first-rate land, [a] proportion of Grove Prairie settled three years since at Government prices; the owner now refuses $4,000 for it.

This region, like the land near Chicago, was originally the home of the Potawatomi people.

The 1851 map (previous page) shows Plainfield happily located at the junction of two major roads: the "Ottawa and Chicago Road," which our traveler followed; and a second road connecting Oswego and Joliet. The town's position on the Du Page River also contributed to its attraction.

Plainfield Exchange, where our traveler stopped for the night, was apparently a way station or hotel beside the River du Page in the settlement of Plainfield.

His description of Plainfield as a portion of 'Grove Prairie' is likely a variation on 'Walker's Grove,' the original name for the area. Walker's Grove was named after either early settler James Walker, or his father-in-law, Rev. Jesse Walker, who established a Methodist mission here to minister to the Potowatomi in 1826. James Walker erected sawmill in 1828, and began claiming land.

In 1832, just three years before our traveler's visit to Plainfield, Native American efforts to reclaim their homelands in the Black Hawk War led Plainfield settlers to hunker down at 'Fort Beggs,' a temporarily-fortified cabin. A few days later, the terrified group left and sought protection at Ft. Dearborn.

The Illinois and Michigan Canal, which would open in 1848, largely followed the Des Plaines River and wended its way through Rockport (east of Plainfield). As a consequence, Plainfield began to wane. The town continued to play an important role in history, however, serving as a sheltering stop for runaway slaves on the Underground Railroad.

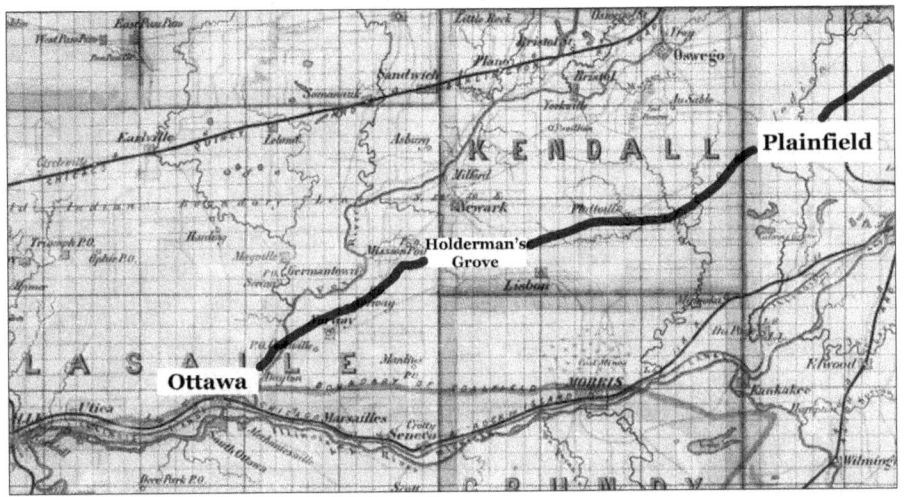

Excerpt of 1861 map of Illinois by L. Richter. (Library of Congress).

June 13:

Half past five, got under way [*leaving Plainfield*].

Bogged our horses and pulled them out. Reached Platt's half-way house on good prairie and breakfasted at nine.

Half past 3, arrived at Holderman's Grove, took b[*rea*]d and milk and proceeded. This Grove is beautiful. Land as good as need be. In coming to [*it*], found the road very bad; had to get out and water nearly knee deep.

Mistook the road and went considerably out of the way. Arrived at Ottawa, [*Illinois*] at 11 o'clock [*p.m.*], after crossing and re-crossing the Illinois; found very inferior accommodations.

The half-way house mentioned by our traveler was three and a half hours' ride from Plainfield. Confusingly, there is also a halfway house in Plainfield (now on the National Register). But this seems to be a different "half-way house" he's referring to, given its distance from Plainfield.

Another five or six hours of travel brought our diarist to Holderman's Grove. Abram (or Abraham) Holderman, his wife Charlotte, and 11 children had arrived at this spot in Big Grove Township, Kendall County, Illinois on October 31, 1831.

Other settlers had arrived and made land claims before him. But Holderman, a wealthy man, was able to quickly buy out multiple land claims, assembling a large tract for himself that included a beautiful grove of black walnut trees.

Abram Holderman (Find-a-Grave).

That particular stand of trees had previously been dubbed "Hawley's Grove," after Pierce Hawley and his family, who'd arrived in the mid-1820s. But it soon became known as "Holderman's Grove," and that was the place name that would stick.

Holderman established the first post office in the county in April, 1834. An inn and tavern at Holderman's Grove also served stage travelers.

Born in 1781, Holderman was in his mid-50s when our traveler came through in 1835. He would die in May, 1861 at the ripe old age of 80, and was buried in the Holderman & Hoge Cemetery in neighboring Grundy County, Illinois.

A Traveler's Diary from 1835

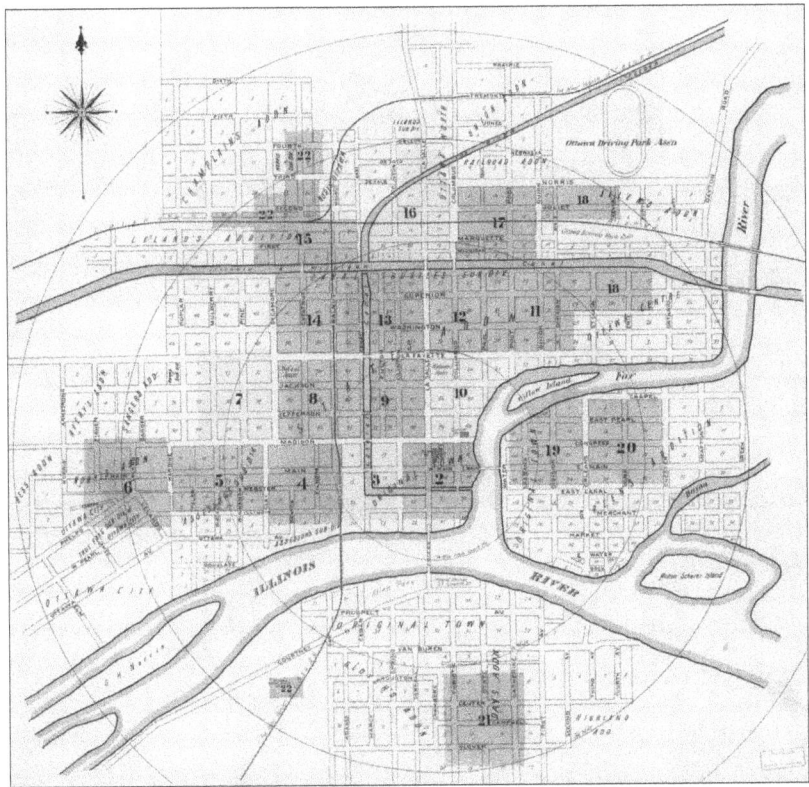

This 1891 Sanborn map of Ottawa shows the confluence of the Fox and Illinois Rivers. The intersecting shaded lines are canals, which (as our writer predicted) later came in on the north side of the river. (Library of Congress).

June 14 - [Sunday]:

Went to Church and viewed the place [*Ottawa*]. The Fox River empties into the Illinois at this place. Directly opposite, on the south side of the Ottawa River, is the best site for a Town. It is a high bluff from which you have a commanding view of the adjacent country.

The scenery is very fine; each point [*of land*] opposite made by [*bends in*] the Fox River has claims for a town, it [*being*] expected the canal will come in on this side. They have a Log Fort built during the recent Indian warfare; also [*a*] Log Jail, which is without a tenant.

39

A Traveler's Diary from 1835

This sketch of Ottawa shows a large, columned house overlooking the river, built by John Hossack in 1854-1855. (Public domain).

[*The following letter, written in the back of the diary and upside down to the rest, was written at Ottawa on this same date. It is included here for chronological consistency.*]

Ottawa, June 14

Messrs. S.J. Robinson

Gent[*lemen*]:

    I promised to let you hear from me when I got out in this western world. We arrived here last evening, after encountering many more difficulties and indignities, [*and*] much more fatigue than I had anticipated, much or the most of it owing to the great travel and bad roads. I refer you to the Messrs. Buckley and Sturgis for particulars as far as Tecumseh, where they left me to proceed on with Mr. Russell, he [*Sturgis*] in vomiting condition. I presume they are with you and have told a bad story before this. I heard from them through Mr. Henck, and was pleased to learn Mr. Sturgis had got better.

After leaving them, we had an intolerable bad road for twelve or fifteen miles when it began to grow better, and some part of it to Niles was as fine as man need ever wish to travel. We got but two or three hours regular sleep, in consequence of the horses being completely worn out. We got into Niles, remained there two days, took the steamboat to the mouth of the St. Joseph and crossed the Lake immediately, with a fine breeze.

They told us at Chicago we could neither get away nor find a place to stay there. We succeeded, however, five of us, in chartering an old box of a wagon, destitute of seats and everything to make it comfortable. We started, rode in the rain, waded through mud and water where the horses could not draw us. Beat out [*exhausted*] our team, chartered and proceeded with another. Got lost last night, went about three miles out of our way, up to our knees in mud and water, the wagon and baggage being quite as much as the horses could get along with.

With all the perplexity, fatigue and hard fare, I have never regretted starting. I have seen the country entirely different from any idea I had ever formed of it. I cannot attempt a description, but I have been fully compensated in the variety I have seen for all the trouble and time expended.

As it regards purchasing lands, it is not to be done, or anything near as I had expected. The country is completely inundated with speculators, selling [*property*] from Maine to anywhere you please. A stranger can get no correct information without he spends much time here. All the lands that are most desirable is [*already*] claimed by preemption; if it is not, they will tell you it is. It would be a great rarity if a man should get hold of the truth respecting a piece of Government land in traveling from Chicago.

Alto[*gether*], I have seen much to admire and much to dislike. I shall keep on, and hope by the time I get through the State to be satisfied to come here to live, or leave it with pleasure.

If you have not sold my rice and there should be any appearance of the march laying claim, I wish you to dispose of it before they get a preemption.

A Traveler's Diary from 1835

With its fortuitous location at the junction of the Fox and Illinois Rivers, it's little wonder that Ottawa was an early trading site. The name Ottawa itself is said to derive from the Native American word 'Awdawe,' which meant 'to trade.'

White trappers and traders showed up about 1823. The town of Ottawa was platted in 1830, just five years before our traveler arrived. Rich nearby farm land and work on the Illinois and Michigan Canal, which began in 1836, would soon attract additional settlers. By 1850, Ottawa would boast a population of roughly 5,000.

The log fort that our writer mentions was Fort Ottawa (later, Fort Johnson), constructed by militia volunteers in 1832 during the Black Hawk War. There are currently no remains or markers to commemorate Ottawa's early fort, but it is believed to have been west of the current interection of State Highways 23 and 71.

This was Abraham Lincoln territory, although our traveler had no way of knowing that his path had crossed that of a future president. On May 27, 1832, Lincoln was mustered out of the service at Ottawa's Fort. (Lincoln would later re-enlist twice for short additional stints before treaties finally ended the Black Hawk War in September that same year.) And in yet another 'claim to fame' for Ottawa's association with Lincoln: the first of the famous Lincoln-Douglas Debates would be held here in August, 1858.

It's unclear what our diarist meant about his "rice" and the threat of "the march laying claim." But the reference to 'preemption' suggests he is talking not just about barrels of rice, but rather about land: possibly a rice plantation somewhere in the South. Although South Carolina was especially famous for its rice plantations, rice was also grown commercially before the Civil War in northeastern and central Georgia.

As this entry was being written, the Cherokee were being pressed to vacate their lands east of the Mississippi River. Hundreds of Cherokee Indians would gather the following month (July, 1835) at a plantation near Calhoun, Georgia to discuss the terms of a proposed removal treaty with the U.S. Commissioner for Indian Affairs. If word of the Native Americans' movements had already reached our diary writer, it's possible this might be the "march" that our diarist mentions.

At that initial meeting in July, the Cherokee would not be pleased with the treaty terms that were offered. They rejected that proposed treaty in October, 1835, but a revised treaty would ostensibly be signed in December, 1835 at New Echota, Georgia. This second treaty, however, was not approved by the Cherokee National Council. It would be amended again, and finally ratified in March, 1836.

Sadly, the Treaty of New Echota would launch the painful forced relocation of over 16,000 Cherokee between 1836-1839 in the infamous "Trail of Tears," during which an estimated 4,000 Cherokee lost their lives.

The high, rocky bluff known as Starved Rock, as it appeared about 1914. (Library of Congress).

June 15:

Paid fare at Ottawa and left in [a] wagon for Utica [*Illinois*], an incorporated city with one house and [a] hog pen, ten miles below Ottawa.

Forded several streams with some danger, besides getting very wet.

Here we have no stages, can get no team, but have to wait the arrival of the Steam Boat.

Viewed Starved Rock a few miles above this, 250 feet high. On this rock the Foxes, Sauks and Potawatomis starved the Illinois Indians.

From Ottawa, our traveler would have headed straight west to reach the early settlement at Utica. The "house and hog pen" he describes <u>may</u> have belonged to Simon Crosair, the first settler at "Old Utica." (Later development would create a "New Utica" a mile or so to the north.)

Crosair established a store and warehouse "for storage and commission business" on the north bank of the Illinois River in 1834. He later captained his own steamboat, operating it on the river.

A history of La Salle County from 1877 confirms the danger that early travelers faced in crossing streams.

> "Traveling unworked roads and crossing streams without bridges was often a perilous adventure. Many were the hair-breadth escapes which most of the early settlers can recall. . . It was a common remark that when a man left home in the morning, it was very uncertain whether his wife's next dress would be a black one, or of some other color."

"Starved Rock" is a large, rocky bluff on the south bank of the river, opposite Utica. Three of its sides are nearly vertical, and the river flows at its base. A steeply winding path on the fourth side led to the flat top, making the rock a nearly impregnable fortress.

According to legend, in 1769 an Illinois warrior killed a leader of the Ottawa tribe. Eager for revenge, the Ottawa and their allies, the Potawatomi, chased a small band of Illinois Indians to the top of this rock and then laid seige, cutting off food and water to the Illinois at the top. According to this legend, when thirst and starvation finally forced the small band of Illinois to surrender, they were killed. An early version of this legend was published by Henry Schoolcraft in 1825.

Today, Starved Rock is an Illinois State Park.

The town of Hennepin was still quite new when our traveler visited in 1835. This substantial five-bedroom brick home on East Mulberry would be built just two years later, in 1837. (Public domain).

June 16:

Here we are [*at Utica*] in more dirt and filth than I ever before witnessed, and no getting away.

    Paid fare at Utica - $1.12-1/2

    Paid Russell for fare at sundry times – 12.25

Five o'clock [*a.m.*], took Steamboat *Banner* for Peoria, [*Illinois*].

Eight [*a.m.*], stopped at Hennepin for wood. Detained two or three hours, and got but very little.

Touched all along shore during the [*day*]; purchased [*fence*] rails in some instances, stole them in others.

A Traveler's Diary from 1835

If our traveler had known the history of the Steamboat Banner, he might have thought twice about stepping on board. A collapsed flue had scalded the engineer in spring 1834, and a chamber maid who jumped overboard in the excitement was thought to have drowned.

Just six months later, in late September, 1834, the Banner's boiler exploded, tearing away

> A Cincinnatti paper of the 4th inst. states that the steamboat Banner collapsed her flue, on the 23d ult. 27 miles below St Louis. The engineer was badly scalded—the chamber maid has not been heard of since, and it is believed that she jumped overboard and was drowned.

Newspaper mention of an accident aboard the Steamboat Banner in 1834 (Vermont Courier, March 21, 1834).

> The steamboat *Banner* exploded on the Mississippi about three weeks since, by which five persons were instantly killed, and 13 badly scalded or wounded. The boat had been stopped for a moment, and the explosion happened on starting again—she was much wrecked, and also took fire—but was run ashore, and all the passengers, including the wounded and the dead, were safely landed.

A second, deadlier accident involving the Banner occurred just six months later. (Niles National Register, St. Louis, Missouri, October 18, 1834).

much of the boiler deck and starting a fire. Five people were killed in the accident and 13 injured, including its captain, Capt. Evans. But the Banner had been repaired and placed back in service by the time our traveler boarded in June, 1835.

Hennepin's history began in 1817, when a pair of trading posts were erected by the American Fur Company and trader Thomas Hartzell about a mile north of the current townsite.

Putnam County was established in January, 1831, and the first house in Hennepin was erected that same year. A townsite was quickly laid out, consisting of 12 – soon to be 20 – blocks. The town's name honored Fr. Louis Hennepin, a Franciscan priest who'd been an early explorer of the region in 1679-80.

When our traveler's steamboat stopped at Hennepin in 1835, the crew was searching for wood to stoke its boilers. Just why wood supplies were slim there is a bit of a mystery, but perhaps it had to do with the size of the town; Hennepin had a population of only about 200 when the Banner made its three-hour stop.

Hennepin's columned Putnam County Courthouse would be completed just a few years later; it was built in 1837 (or some sources say 1839). *This beautiful building still stands, and today is the oldest still-active courthouse in Illinois. It is listed on the National Register of Historic Places.*

After leaving Hennepin, the Banner continued steaming its way along the Illinois River, still searching for wood. Where commercial wood supplies weren't available, the crew evidently tore down local fences and burned those instead. It probably wasn't an uncommon practice. One can only imagine how angry local farmers must have been as they repeatedly repaired their fence lines!

Putnam County's historic courthouse (eBay).

Peoria as it looked in 1831, by J.M. Roberts (from 1873 Atlas Map of Peoria County). The small building to the far left is identified as the "courthouse." (Courtesy of Peoria Historical Society Collection/Bradley University Library.)

June 17:

Morning, touched at Rome. House and [a] half in the place. Number [of] inhabitants not ascertained.

Arrived at Peoria, [*Illinois*], very pleasantly situated.

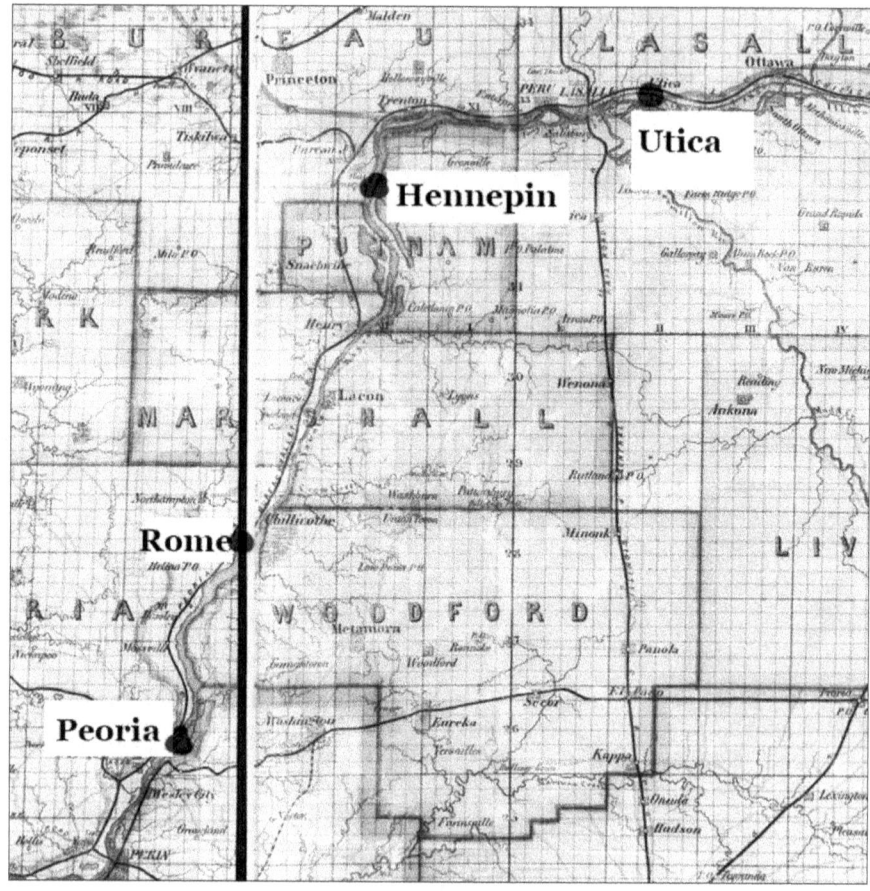

L. Richter map of Illinois, 1861 (Library of Congress).

By now our traveler's steamboat had made the great bend in the Illinois River and was chugging south toward St. Louis.

The town of Rome, Illinois consisted of just a "house and a half" when he arrived. Peoria, by contrast, was home to about 1,600 people when our traveler paid his 1835 visit. It was incorporated that same year.

The original inhabitants in this region were the Peoria Indians, one of the principal tribes in the Illinois (Illini) Confederacy, which in turn was part of the Algonquin Nation. About 1768, following inter-tribal warfare, the Kickapoo took possession and settled here.

A Traveler's Diary from 1835

Peoria was the first European settlement in the future state of Illinois. As European explorers and settlers arrived, a series of forts was established here. The first was "Fort Crevecoeur," built on the east side of the river in 1680 by French explorers. "Fort Pimiteoui" followed, built in 1691 west of the river, where the city later developed. Fort Clark was built in 1813 and, after Peoria County was formed in 1825, was renamed "Peoria" – the name the city bears today.

Peoria incorporated as a town in 1835, the same year our traveler arrived. Construction began that same year on two important civic improvements: a courthouse and a jail. Thatis was apparently not the <u>first</u> courthouse, however; the town had had a small wooden courthouse as early as 1831, according to a contemporary sketch. Peoria would officially become a city in 1845.

Among Peoria's future "claims to fame": Abraham Lincoln and Stephen Douglas would deliver speeches about slavery on the Peoria courthouse steps in 1859. And you probably have heard the familiar question, "Yes, but will it play in Peoria?" That expression was taken from Horatio Alger's 1890 novel, <u>Five Hundred Dollars</u>, in which "playing at Peoria" meant achieving a level of acceptability in mainstream America.

The Courthouse at Peoria. Inset from Daniel B. Allen map of Peoria, Illinois, 1861 (Library of Congress).

The Flanagan House in Peoria was built in 1837, just two years after our traveler's visit. Today it is the oldest residence still standing, located at 942 N.E. Glen Oak, Peoria, Illinois. (Courtesy of Peoria Historical Society Collection/Bradley University Library.)

June 18 and 19:

>1 handkerchief
>2 shirts
>1 pair drawers
>5 col[lar]s
>3 pair stockings

On horseback, set out for Tremont. After passing over good road, bad road, through mud and water, sunshine and rain, reached there about one o'clock.

Spent ten or fifteen minutes in viewing the place [*Tremont*]; ascertained we could get neither refreshments for ourselves, which we needed very much, or feed for our horses.

A Traveler's Diary from 1835

Made for the first probable House for procuring something to eat, succeeded in getting [a] glass of milk, cold bacon, and bread; nothing for the horses.

Traveled back several miles before we could procure something for the horses to eat. Succeeded in getting back to Peoria the next morning [*June 19, at*] 10 o'clock.

June 19: Spent in viewing different farms in the vicinity of Peoria. Mr. Russell purchased.

The town of Tremont, Illinois is located about a dozen miles southeast of Peoria. Its name reflects the presence of three mounds (trimounts) nearby, which interrupt the otherwise-flat pairie.

Our traveler mentioned encountering muddy roads and standing water on his ride to Tremont. The spring and summer of 1835 experienced unusually heavy rainstorms. The untilled prairie collected the water, at times forming "one vast lake." One especially heavy rainstorm in early July would be long remembered for its thunder, lightning, and violent downpour. Sadly, all that standing water soon became a breeding ground for disease.

The town of Tremont was just getting off the ground when our traveler arrived. Indian traders had located in the vicinity in 1826, and James Sterling and William Broyhill, the first permanent white settlers, arrived in Tremont Township with their families in 1830.

Other families from the east quickly began to settle here as well. In 1833, Josiah James and his friend, John Harris, persuaded friends in New York City to relocate here and form a colony. Some 40 or 50 souls packed up their possessions and arrived by wagon in 1834. They quickly laid out a townsite, and built a church and a school.

It was just the next year when our diary writer and his friend visited Tremont in June, 1835. Town lots had only been parceled out to the eager settlers that February, so the town was still brand new. Little wonder, then, that our visitors chafed at finding no place to get food for themselves or their horses. Local history says a two-

story wooden tavern was built at Tremont in 1835; but perhaps it had not yet been finished by the time they arrived.

On July 25, 1835, only weeks after our traveler's brief visit, the town held a vote and decided to incorporate.

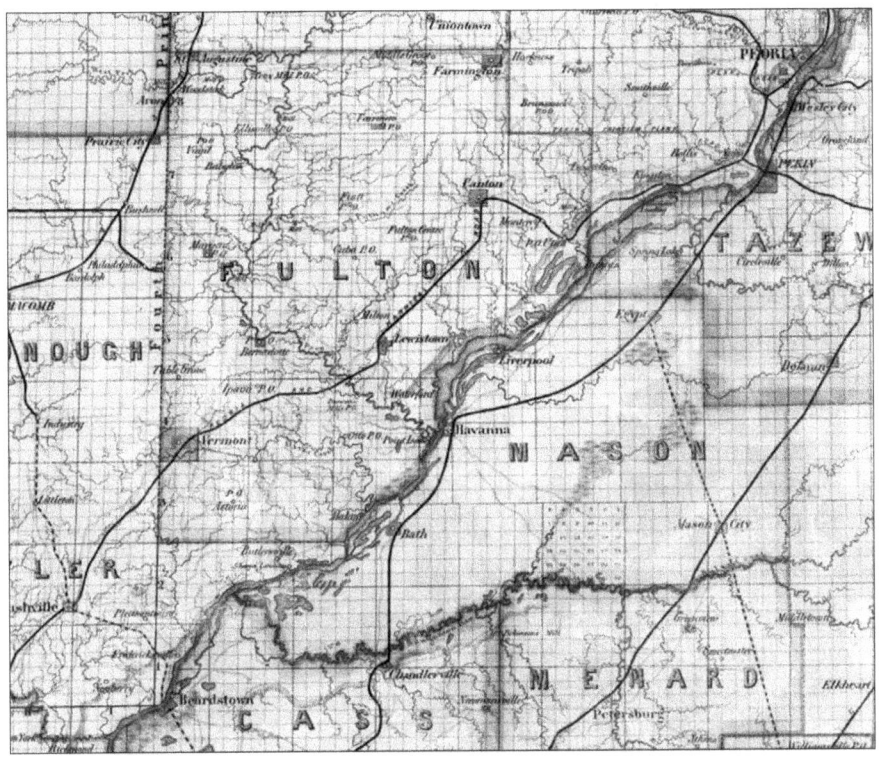

Excerpt from 1861 L. Richter map of Illinois, showing Peoria at top right, with Pekin just below it. Beardstown is at lower left. (Library of Congress).

June 20:

Took Steamboat *Friendship* for St. Louis.

Touched at Pekin to receive freight. Population about 500; very sickly, cold, dreary-looking place. It commands a better and much more settled back country than Peoria.

Arrived at Beardstown, [*Illinois*] in the night.

Highlighting the dangers of steamboat travel: the Friendship would collide with the Steamboat American the following year (1836), causing the other vessel to sink and drowning several of its passengers.

> The St. Louis Bulletin of the 22d ult states, that the steamboats American and Friendship came in contact on the Illinois river the Wednesday previous. The American sunk almost instantly. Several persons are missing, supposed to be drowned—names unknown. The Friendship suffered no injury.

Bangor Daily Whig & Courier, August 12, 1836.

Pekin when our traveler arrived was indeed an "sickly, cold, dreary-looking place." At least one other diary similarly describes "uncommonly wet, soggy weather," with heavy thunderstorms, hailstorms, lightning and even frost that May and June. There had also been an outbreak of cholera, likely due to all the standing water.

Pekin's first permanent white settler had been Jonathan Tharp, who built a log cabin in 1824 on the east side of the river. A Native American village of about one hundred wigwams stood just to the north of Tharp's cabin, inhabited by Potawatomi Chief Shaubena and his tribe.

Tharp began farming a large tract of land (an area that would later become downtown Pekin), and developed a friendship with his Native American neighbors. Tharp's father (Jacob), family members, and a friend joined him in 1825, and built cabins nearby. Other settlers soon followed.

The first steamboat stopped at Pekin in 1828. Local legend has it

Jacob Tharp, father of Pekin founder Jonathan Tharp. Jacob would have been living in Pekin at the time our traveler visited. (Photo originally published in Pekin, Illinois Sesquicentennial (1824 - 1974) - A History).

that the elder Tharp (Jacob) was so shocked by the unfamiliar shriek of the steamboat's whistle that he thought it was the Angel Gabriel, blowing his trumpet for Judgment Day!

The Tharps were the first to attempt to plot out a town. But they found little interest in their new townsite at first. In 1829 a different surveyor created a new townsite plat. Rights to that plat were auctioned off at Springfield that same year, and lots were sold in 1830.

A humorous story is told about competing bidders at that 1829 Springfield auction. One fiery determined bidder," armed to the eyebrows," offered $1.25 an acre for the new townsite and threatened to shoot anyone who bid against him. Not surprisingly, he strode out of the auction house as the nominal winner. But disgruntled competitor Major Isaac Perkins and friends promptly "captured the usurper," whisked him away to a quiet location, and "persuaded" him to sign over his title to the coveted land.

The Tharps had originally wanted to christen their new town 'Cincinnati.' But 'Pekin' was the final choice. Apocryphal stories say that the town's name was selected by Ann Eliza Cromwell, wife of one of the town's developers, who either believed the new town lay directly opposite Peking, China on the globe, or hoped it would someday rival Peking in size and prominence. Settler Jacob Tharp's diary similarly referred to the new Illinois town as "the Celestial City."

This postcard shows dock workers loading and unloading a later-model steamboat at Beardstown, Illinois, circa 1900.

June 21:

Detained here [*at Beardstown*] taking freight. This place [*has*] 500 inhabitants, more sound houses and business appearances than any place I have seen in the State.

It lays low. At this stage of the river, which is very high, you can see nothing on the off-side of the river but the tops of trees above water, which is the case all along the river.

At this time, the place is deserted by the inhabitants. Seven cases and two deaths yesterday by cholera.

Oppressively hot one day, chilling cold with overcoats on the next. Thermometer ranging [*from*] 68 to 100.

A Traveler's Diary from 1835

By 1874, Beardstown would boast many fine homes, like this residence owned by Thomas H. Carter. (Illustrated Atlas Map of Cass County (1874), Library of Congress).

Half past 8 [*a.m.*]: passed Meredosia, suppose 150 or 200 inhabitants, apparently [a] farming community.

Nine [*a.m.*], passed Naples: Twenty houses, rather more respectable in appearance than in any other town passed on the River.

Touched through the day at several small places for freight, passengers, wood, &tc.; in the night, arrived at Alton. Remained there until seven next morning.

Beardstown was established by Thomas Beard, a native of Granville, New York, who built a log cabin there in 1819. Beard traded with the local Indians, and launched a ferry service across the river in 1826. He platted the town in 1829.

Beardstown became a popular port, from which goods like hogs and grain raised on local farms would be shipped downriver. The town was once known as "the belle at the bend" thanks to its location at a bend in the Illinois River. As stockyards and slaughterhouses were built, Beardstown also won the less-attractive moniker of "Porkopolis."

As our traveler observed, peak high water would often come in June — the month our traveler came through. High water would continue to bring flooding problems for Beardstown residents. An old photo from October, 1922, for example, shows Beardstown residents standing thigh-deep in water in the middle of State Street. Today, Beardstown has a 35-foot flood wall to help protect the town.

Cholera was one of the most feared and fatal diseases of the 19th century. A severe bacterial infection leading to rapid dehydration and frequently death, cholera was transmitted through contaminated water or food.

The end often came quickly for victims. "To meet a man at night and attend his funeral in the morning has ceased to alarm, much less to surprise," wrote one observer. "Some die in three hours; seldom do they live twelve, and very rarely twenty-four."

Cholera began to ravage Illinois towns in 1832, when federal troops brought the disease with them during the Black Hawk War. Successive epidemics struck again in 1833 and 1834. And, as we see from our traveler's diary, deaths due to cholera continued in 1835.

No one yet understood that the epidemic was caused by a bacteria. But people _did_ understand that proximity to those infected had something to do with catching it. Fleeing town in an effort to escape the contagion was common. Roughly half the population of New York City fled to the countryside during a cholera outbreak in 1832, for example. It's thus not surprising that our traveler found Beardstown "deserted by the inhabitants," given its recent outbreak.

As our traveler continued downriver, he passed Meredosia and Naples. According to some sources, Meredosia was named after a French priest, Antoine D'Osia, whose cabin was found here as early as 1816. Others say, however, that "osia" referred to willows growing nearby.

Meredosia was just beginning to grow when our diarist visited. A general store had opened in 1832, and the townsite had been surveyed that same year. In 1835, the year our diarist arrived, both a whiskey distillery and a blacksmith shop were added to the town's amenities. Our traveler was probably right in his estimate of 150 to 200 residents; Meredosia would double in the coming years to a population of 414 in the 1860 census.

Naples is thought to have taken its name from Naples, Italy. It was founded about 1825. Sadly, members of the Potawatomi tribe on the "Trail of Death" would cross there in 1838 during their forced relocation.

Naples was tiny when our traveler viewed it in 1835: just twenty houses. It still hasn't grown much bigger; the 2000 Census recorded only 45 households (134 people) living in Naples, Illinois.

The Old Market House and Levee at St. Louis, with steamship shown at right. (James Kershaw map, ca. 1848), Library of Congress).

June 22:

Alton, [*Illinois*] is on very hilly and uneven ground, buildings mostly of stone. Four churches, the first seen in this state. [*They are*] building [*a*] penitentiary.

[*Alton*] is probabl[y] the most [*attractive*] and likely will be the greatest place for business in the State, excepting Chicago, which can never be what is anticipated at this time.

    Paid Steamboat Fare – $5.00
    L[*aundry*] & Boots – .25, Sundries .75 – [*Total:*] 1.00

Eight [*a.m.*], arrived at St. Louis [*Missouri*]. Situated very well, apparently [*a*] business place and growing. Streets very narrow and rather dirty, sickly [*with*] cholera and bilious fever [*malaria*].

Took Steam Boat *Caledonia* for [*the*] Ohio River. In passing U.S. Arsenal [*Island*] 3 or 4 miles below St. Louis, it makes a very pretty appearance.

Vite Bush [*a phoenetic corruption of 'Poche Vide,' an early name for Carolondelet*], a few miles below the Arsenal, [*is*] about 100 houses, in the midst of bushes and low oaks. The houses about the size and appearance of Carolina negro huts.

[*Jefferson*] Barracks, twelve miles from St. Louis, [*is*] very pleasantly situated in a scattered grove of trees on the Missouri side, which, with the buildings, gives the place a very neat and romantic appearance.

Entered the Ohio River at night.

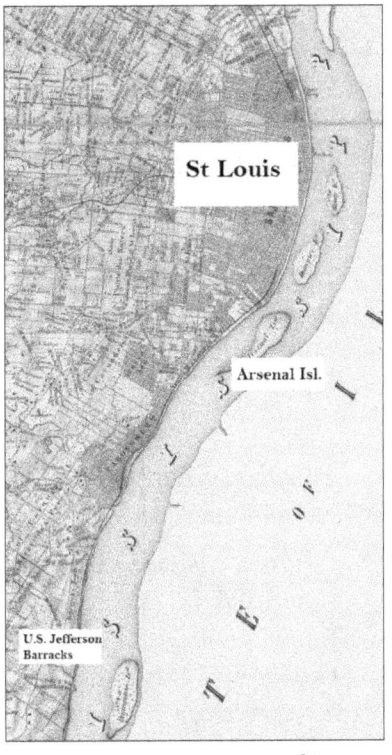

The Caledonia, the steamboat that ferried our traveler downriver, was a sidewheel steamer, built in 1823. In addition to 300 tons of cargo, she had room for 100 or so cabin passengers, and 300 or more "deck passengers."

Gustavus Waagner map of St. Louis, 1857. The island at bottom of the map was called 'Quarantine Island,' a reference to its use during outbreaks of disease. (Library of Congress).

A year later, the Caledonia would make the news when it carried an entire colony of settlers bound for Marion City, Missouri, accompanied by not only household goods such as spinning wheels but also timbers for 25 houses, already "hewn, squared and numbered."

The town of Alton is on the Illinois (east) side of the river, just above St. Louis. Established in 1818, Alton developed as a trading town, making use of its fortunate position at the confluence of three rivers: the Illinois, Missouri, and Mississippi.

St. Louis, as our traveler noted, was a prosperous place indeed in 1835, and still growing. It had achieved early prominence as the capital of Louisiana Territory in 1805, and continued to serve as the capital from 1812 to 1821 after Louisiana Territory was renamed Missouri Territory.

The population of St. Louis jumped from 1,400 residents in 1810 to 4,600 in 1820. Economic activity sagged during the financial Panic of 1819, but by the 1830s commerce was making dramatic strides again. Over the next decade and a half, the population of St. Louis leaped from 5,832 in 1820 to 8,316 in 1835, the year our traveler visited. By 1850 St. Louis would be the second-largest port in the nation, trailing only New York City.

"The Arsenal" was established by the U.S. War Department in 1827 on 37 acres near the river, not far from a military base known as Jefferson Barracks. As the name implies, the Arsenal held weapons and munitions.

Arsenal Island was a large island in the middle of the Mississippi River in 1835. Spring floods would annually chip away at the island's land mass, and erosion accelerated dramaticallly after the City of St. Louis constructed dykes. Most of this island would wash away between 1853 and 1863.

Just below the city of St. Louis was Poche Vide (later Carondelet), also on the Missouri side of the river. Carondelet traces its early history to a French settler who arrived in 1767. It was incorporated as a town in 1832. The predominant language spoken at the time our traveler passed was French Creole. Citizens generally made their living by supplying St. Louis with food and firewood.

Jefferson Barracks, a military training post, was established by the U.S. War Department in 1826 on land that once had been part of the Carondelet village commons. At the time our visitor passed by, recruits were still living in tents; buildings to house them were not completed until 1837. During the Civil War, this installation would become a military hospital.

Not far from the Barracks was Quarantine Island, shown at the bottom of the map on the previous page. As the name implies, it was used to quarantine those with infectious diseases. Arsenal Island (to the north) would also be used for quarantine purposes, beginning with a cholera epidemic in 1849, leading to later confusion between the two islands (especially after much of the northerly island disappeared in the 1850s and early '60s from erosion).

When our traveler passed by, Illinois (east of the river) was a free state. Missouri (on the west), by contrast, had been admitted to the Union fifteen years earlier (March 6, 1820) as a slave state.

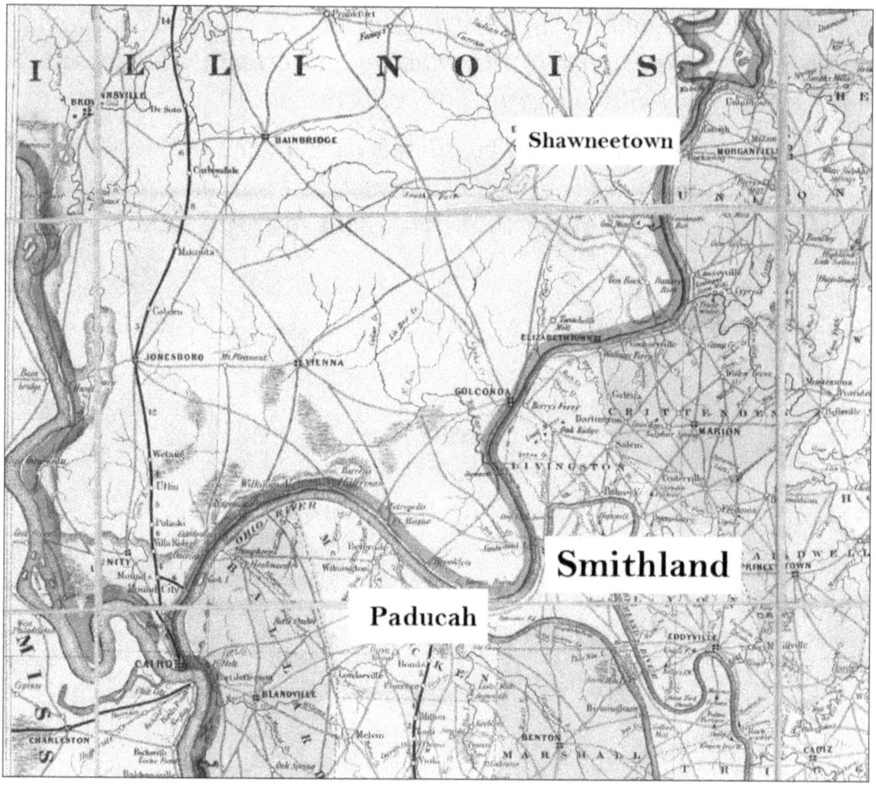

A Traveler's Diary from 1835

After descending the Mississippi River (at left), our traveler's steamboat veered northeast up the Ohio River, touching first at Paducah, Kentucky. (James T. Lloyd map of Kentucky, 1862, from Library of Congress).

June 23:

7 o'clock [*a.m.*], touched at Paducah, Kentucky for passengers, at the mouth of the Tennessee River. Quite a neat little place in appearance, probably 600 inhabitants.

Nine [*a.m.*], touched at Smithland at the mouth of the Cumberland River in Kentucky. Four or five hundred inhabitants, sixty miles from [*the*] mouth of the Ohio. Cholera has prevailed here, but not much at this time.

A Traveler's Diary from 1835

Seven [*p.m.*], passed Shawneetown, [*Illinois*], ten miles from [*the*] mouth of Wabash River, quite a pretty little place. Very level but rather low, said to be sickly.

An 1857 sketch of Cairo, the southernmost town in Illinois, where our traveler made the bend into the Ohio River. A steamboat is shown in the foreground at right. (Illustration by Jnst. Arnst & Co. (Library of Congress).

Paducah, Kentucky was settled about 1815, and thrived due to its position at the confluence of the Ohio and Tennessee Rivers. The town was incorporated in 1830, and in 1832 became the county seat of McCracken County.

Smithland, Kentucky sits on a bluff above the Ohio River, and was named for early explorer James Smith. A 14-room inn known as the Gower House, built in 1780 and operated by Stanley P. Gower, was standing in Smithland when our traveler passed by, and is still visible from the outside today (now on the National Register of Historic Places, and privately-owned). A log cabin, constructed at approximately the same time as our traveler's visit (sometime between 1834-36) also still stands in Smithland, and is now known as the Livingston County Historic Log Cabin Museum.

As our traveler observed, cholera had broken out before his arrival, though the epidemic had not been as severe as a previous contagion that had swept through in 1833, two years earlier.

Shawneetown, Illinois may have been established as early as 1758. As the name implies, it once was home to a large settlement of the Shawnee tribe, occupying both sides of the river. A town was laid out by white settlers in 1810, and it became a prominent entry point to Illinois for settlers. A land office opened in 1812, and a bank in 1816. In 1830, the population of the town was 446; by 1840 it would more than triple in size, to 1,900 people.

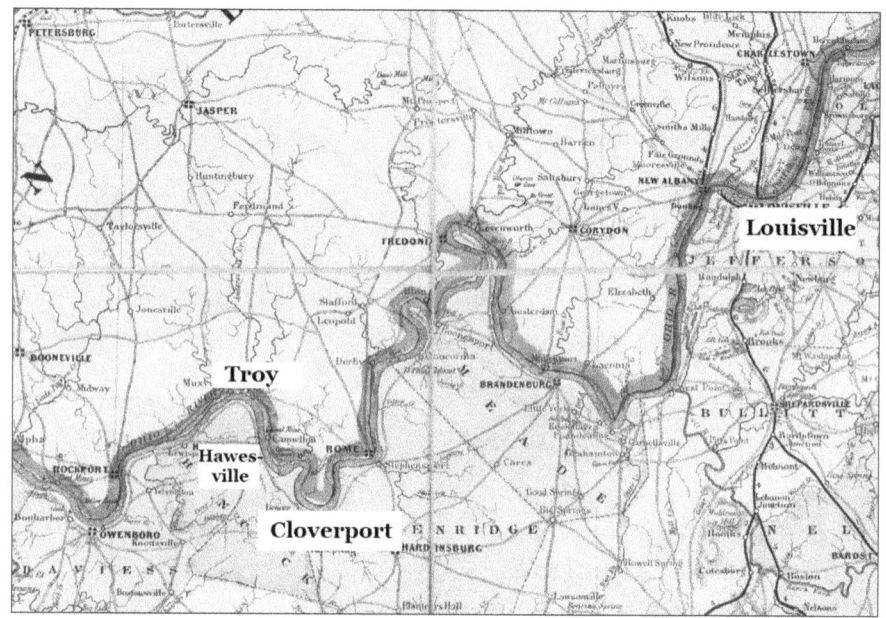

As he steamed east along the Ohio River, our traveler straddled Indiana to the north and Kentucky to the south. (James T. Lloyd map of Kentucky, 1862, from Library of Congress).

June 24:

Rainy day and hard current to contend with.

One o'clock [*p.m.*], passed Troy, Indiana, [*a*] rather rusty-looking place.

Two, passed Hawesville, a hard-looking place on [*the*] Kentucky shore, say 25 houses with a courthouse; [*they*] look more like North Carolina cribs than good houses.

Half past three, passed Cloverport, about thirty houses [*on the*] Kentucky side. Quite a neat, rural-looking little place.

Seven [*p.m.*], stopped [*on the*] Indiana side and charged well with wood.

Several on the sick list; medicine chest and medical aid none too good for such times.

Louisville [*is*] 100 miles distant.

Some say Troy is Indiana's second-oldest community, after Vincennes (though others give that honor to Indianapolis). Troy became the county seat of Perry County in 1816, and a post office opened there as early as 1818.

Hawesville, Kentucky was named for Richard Hawes, Sr., who donated land to create a county seat for Hancock County in 1829. A post office opened in Hancock County the same year. A ferry across the river between Kentucky and Indiana began in 1831.

In 1830, all of Hancock County had just 190 households. But it quickly became a center of local commerce. Steamboats were built here, and coal was also sold to fuel the steamers that plied the river.

The city of Hawesville was formed in 1836, a year after our traveler's visit. During its boom years, Hawesville was indeed a "hard" place, known "for the best saloons and gambling games in the region," as one later historian put it.

The early courthouse our traveler mentions seeing would become the backdrop for a famous shoot-out in March of 1859, when competing factions (led respectively by a local merchant and the district prosecutor) traded bullets. The dramatic confrontation even made the pages of Harper's Weekly. A newer courthouse would be built in 1867.

Kentucky was a slave state when our traveler visited, and it's entirely possible that some of the poorer homes he viewed were slave quarters. In the coming years, although Kentucky officially tried to remain neutral, many Hawesville residents favored the Confederacy. Richard Hawes, Jr., son of the town's founder, would become Kentucky's second Confederate governor in 1862, after some Kentucky representatives voted to secede from the Union.

During the Civil War Hawesville became a refuge for Confederate guerillas, preying on Union forces and supplies. As a result, the town was shelled repeatedly by Union cannons and gunboats.

Located at a bend in the Ohio River, Cloverport, Kentucky and its sheltering hills offered safe mooring for ships. Cloverport got its start with an early settlement on the upper side of Clover Creek, possibly named for abundant wild clover growing near by. This early settlement was known as "Joe's Landing" (and later "Joeville") after Joe Huston, who settled here in 1798, and operated a ferry across the river.

Cloverport started on the lower side of the same creek, and a post office opened there in 1828. The two communities merged in the mid-1860s.

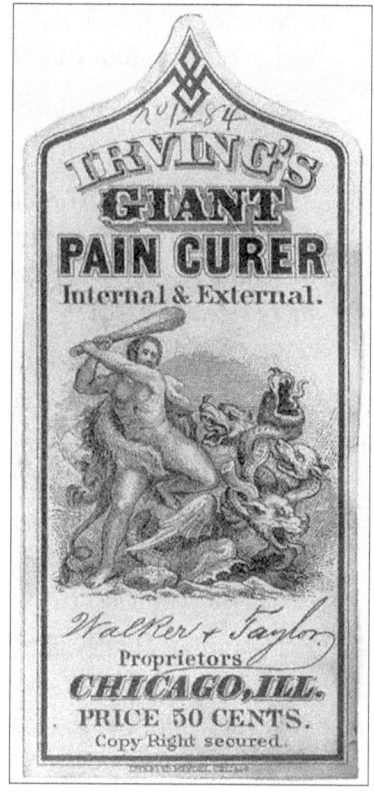

It's unclear what remedies the steamboat's "medicine chest" contained, but patent remedies (many of which contained opium) might have been included. This patent medicine, made in Chicago, was available circa 1830-1870. (Library of Congress).

A Traveler's Diary from 1835

Some 70 years after our traveler passed through the lock, this 1906 photo captured a steamboat in the Louisville Canal. (Detroit Publishing Co., Library of Congress).

June 25:

Half past 8 [*a.m.*], passed New Albany, Indiana. Apparently [*a*] smart, growing place of about 1,500 or 2,000 inhabitants. [At] nine, entered Lock in [*the*] Canal for Louisville, [*KY*].

This Canal two miles through; [*it*] is called Louisville & Portland Canal, dug through solid rock most of the way. Cost nearly one million [*dollars*]. Lowest stage of the River [*is*] 3 feet of water, highest upwards of twenty. The stone taken from it lies piled up on either side from ten to 40 foot high.

Louisville – much business transacted here. Apparently growing and flourishing. Streets [*are*] paved, or rather stoned, in good, solid condition. Population nineteen thousand. It is

Sketch of Louisville, Kentucky's bustling Main Street in 1846. (National Archives image #513346, Public domain).

said there are four hundred buildings going up at this time. Allow one-half the number, which [is] as near truth as you generally get in this latitutude.

Jeffersonville, opposite, is a pleasant-looking place. They have a canal in contemplation for leading water from the Ohio for manufacturing purposes. A bridge across is also in contemplation, all of which will probably be of importance to Louisville for money-making. I give Louisville the preference to any place I noticed [*thus far*].

Negroes, whiskey, dissipation and gambling abound here. Part of the population very wealthy, and some good society. Finest-looking women seen on the route. Houses not as fine as expected.

Very severe tempest, thunder, lightning, rain in torrents. Not much cholera here. Manhattan (?)(*illegible*) done their best last night.

Louisville, Kentucky was indeed a booming place in 1835. Its population in 1828 had been roughly 7,000; but our traveler's estimate of 19,000 people in 1835 probably wasn't far off. By 1840 it would have more than 21,000 residents.

Early shipping activity had carried goods only downstream on the Ohio River, as it was impractical to fight the current up-river. But with the arrival of steamboats, the economic equation changed. The first steamboat to successfully venture upstream from New Orleans – against the current – reached Louisville in 1815. And soon, of course, others followed.

The other obstacle to river navigation had long been the "falls" near Louisville, which required goods to be off-loaded and hauled overland to avoid the obstruction. The Louisville & Portland Canal was completed around the falls in 1830, allowing steamboats to travel from Pittsburgh in the north to New Orleans in the south (and the reverse).

Sadly, Louisville, Kentucky at the time our traveler arrived was the center for a booming slave trade. By the 1850s, some 2,500 to 4,000 enslaved people each year were sold to slave brokers at Louisville, who in turn shipped these unfortunates to the slave market in New Orleans to serve southern plantations.

Enslaved blacks at Louisville knew they were only a river's width away from freedom. If they could just reach Indiana on the north side of the Ohio River, they had a chance at freedom. The few who managed to successfully escape, however, faced continuing dangers even in the "free" states. These included bounty-hunters eager to catch runaway slaves.

Unlike Hawesville, Louisville would become a major Union stronghold during the Civil War. After the War was over, however, many returning Confederate soldiers took political posts in the city, leading some to joke that Louisville "joined the Confederacy after the war was over."

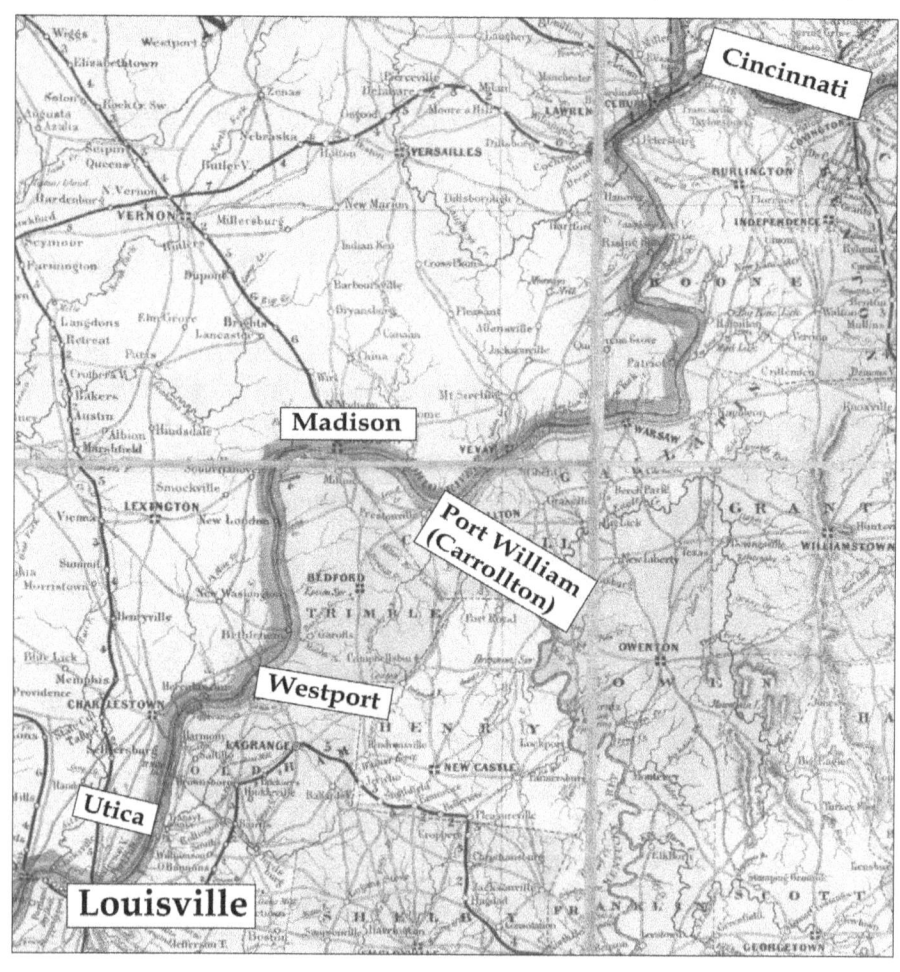

June 26:

Ten o'clock [a.m.], got under way under full power of steam and proceeded on towards Pittsburgh.

Eleven, passed Utica, Indiana. Decent looking little place, about 300 inhabitants. Detained half hour for freight.

Two [p.m.], passed Westport, Kentucky, [the] seat of justice for Oldham County. Old, but said not to improve much. About 200 inhabitants.

At six, passed Madison, Indiana. Here I should have been pleased to remain a day, but the cholera prevailed at this time.

This place [*Madison*] contains 2,200 inhabitants, surrounded almost by bold hills, many of them covered with forest trees that, with the river and another small place opposite on [*the*] Kentucky shore called Milton, makes the scenery at once striking and peculiarly interesting. Here is my home, if a slight and passing view could fix it, in preference to anything seen in the West.

Sundown, passed Little and Big Kentucky Rivers. At the junction of [*the*] latter, Port William [*Carrollton, Kentucky*] is very prettily situated, rather old and apparently not improving much.

I have to regret the loss of daylight; fine evening and country very interesting, in comparison with most passed through.

Leaving Louisville behind, our traveler was wending his way northeast up the Ohio River toward Cincinnati. He was slowly returning to the more-developed world he knew, after adventuring in the sparsely-settled 'west.'

Utica, Indiana had been settled in 1794 by James Noble Wood and his wife. Wood launched a ferry service conveying travelers across the Ohio River, an operation that lasted until 1825.

The town of Utica was laid out in 1816, and named after the New York hometown of the local judge, John Miller. Town organizers contracted with a Louisville carpenter to build 100 log cabins to get the town started, at $25 each. Although Utica grew rapidly for a time, it was eventually eclipsed by nearby Louisville.

Westport, Kentucky was described by our traveler as "old," and he tartly observed that time hadn't improved it much. He was correct about the settlement's age; the town dates to Revolutionary War days, when Elijah Craig obtained a land grant in May, 1780. The tiny settlement was briefly known as "Liberty" before changing its name to "Westport."

A Traveler's Diary from 1835

Panoramic view of Madison, Indiana in 1866. "Here is my home," our traveler wrote in 1835. (Library of Congress).

Settlers began streaming in about 1804, after the Louisiana Territory opened. Thanks to its position on the Ohio River, Westport quickly developed into a thriving commercial town, with bustling steamboat docks and a ferry service connecting to the Indiana side of the river. When Oldham County was formed in 1823, Westport became its county seat, as our traveler noted.

Subsequent years would not be kind to this once-thriving river town, however. When the railroad came through, it bypassed Westport. River commerce also began to dwindle. The 2010 Census would count just 268 residents — fewer even than the 300 who lived here when our traveler viewed Westport from his steamboat, 175 years before.

Madison, Indiana, located at a big bend in the river, really captured our traveler's fancy. "Here is my home," he wrote, "in preference to anything seen in the West." The size of the town, with 2,200 residents at the time of his visit in 1835, may have promised a wealth of business opportunities. (See later photo, previous page).

Madison had been platted in 1810, with the first homes going up the following year. And the next few years after our traveler's visit would, indeed, be prosperous ones for the town. Construction would begin the following year (1836) on the Madison, Indianapolis & Lafayette Railroad. By 1850, Madison would have achieved bragging rights as the third-largest city in Indiana, out-shone only by Indianapolis and New Albany.

But like other cities dependent on river traffic for its growth, Madison would decline as railroad lines sprouted up, drawing commerce away from the Ohio River and eventually making steamboats obsolete.

Our traveler was not nearly as impressed with the next town he came to: Port William, Kentucky. Despite "fine country" nearby, the town itself, he sniffed, was "rather old and apparently not improving much."

Port William, founded in 1794, was indeed somewhat older than the crop of newer towns our traveler had visited. It would be renamed 'Carrollton' in 1838 after Charles Carroll, a signer of the Declaration of Independence.

Had our traveler bothered to disembark from his steamboat, he might have seen the Masterson House in the heart of Port William (now Carrollton, KY). This brick home was built by Richard and Sarah Masterson about 1790, using slave labor. The home has been restored and is now listed on the National Register of Historic Places. It is one of the two oldest surviving homes along the Ohio River west of the Allegheny Mountains. (Photo courtesy of the Port William Historical Society).

A Traveler's Diary from 1835

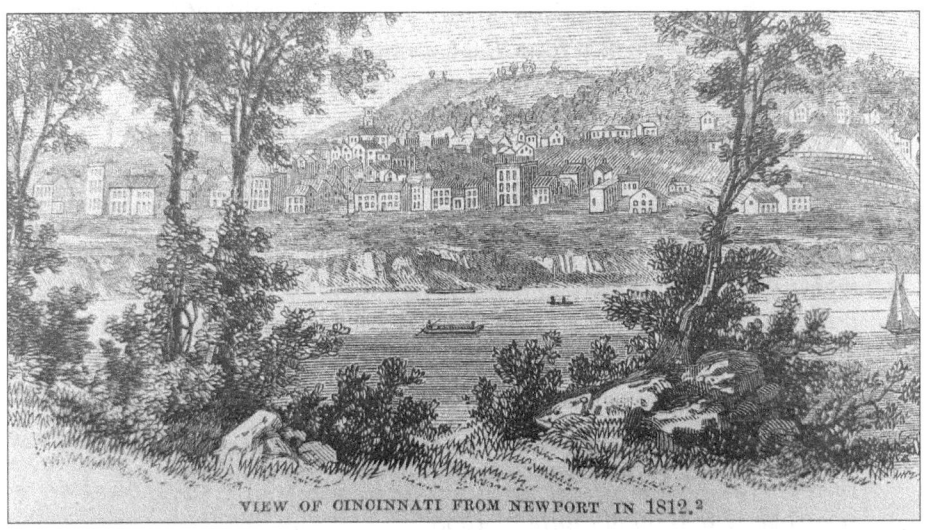

Above: A view of Cincinnati in 1812 from Benson Lossing, "The Pictorial Field Book of the War of 1812." (Public domain).

Below: Portion of a panoramic view of Cincinnati in 1866. (Photo by J.W. Winder, Library of Congress).

June 27:

10 o'clock [a.m.], arrived at Cincinnati, [Ohio]; 32,000 inhabitants.

The town lies well on rising ground. Opposite [are] Newport and [Covington, Kentucky], two neat-looking places. Some cases of cholera.

Six o'clock [p.m.], proceeded on in [Steamboat] *Caledonia* towards Pittsburgh.

A Traveler's Diary from 1835

If our traveler left his steamboat to take in the sights at Cincinnati, he failed to leave us a record. Given the mention of recent cholera cases, it's likely he simply hunkered down aboard.

In 1788, three settlers had launched what would become Cincinnati. The town soon morphed into a substantial shipping port, and it was incorporated in 1819. Dubbed the "Queen of the West," Cincinnati became a major pork processing center and exported hay and other goods. Its growth was assisted in the mid-1820s by the building of the Miami and Erie Canal, which linked Cincinnati with Middletown in 1827 and by 1840 extended as far as Toledo.

The population of Cincinnati was still growing rapidly when our traveler arrived. The city had more than doubled in population between 1810 and 1830, rising from 9,642 to 24,831. Our traveler reported 32,000 inhabitants in 1835.

Days after our traveler's eight-hour visit, a Cincinnati watchmaker named Richard Clayton would attempt an adventurous trip in a hot air balloon, hoping to float all the way to the Atlantic Ocean. His balloon was called "Star of the West," perhaps a twist on Cincinnati's own moniker, "Queen of the West."

Graphic from ad in Cincinnati Daily Gazette, June 29, 1837.

Clayton had already attempted two previous balloon flights. Just three months earlier, he'd soared 350 miles before crash-landing at Keeney's Knob, [West] Virginia. Clayton made it back to Cincinnati by steamboat the following week, but vowed to try again. And try again he did, only to crash-land on top of a Cincinnati building in his second effort.

Undeterred, Clayton attempted his flight yet again, re-launching his balloon on July 4, 1835, only days after our traveler's arrival. This effort, too, was destined to fail; stormy weather and intense

A Traveler's Diary from 1835

cold forced Clayton to bring his balloon to earth again in Pike County, Ohio.

Clayton resumed his occupation as a watch-maker and jeweler in Cincinnati. His store was affectionately known as 'Clayton's Balloon Store.'

But the West Virginia town where he'd crash-landed changed its name to Clayton, in his honor.

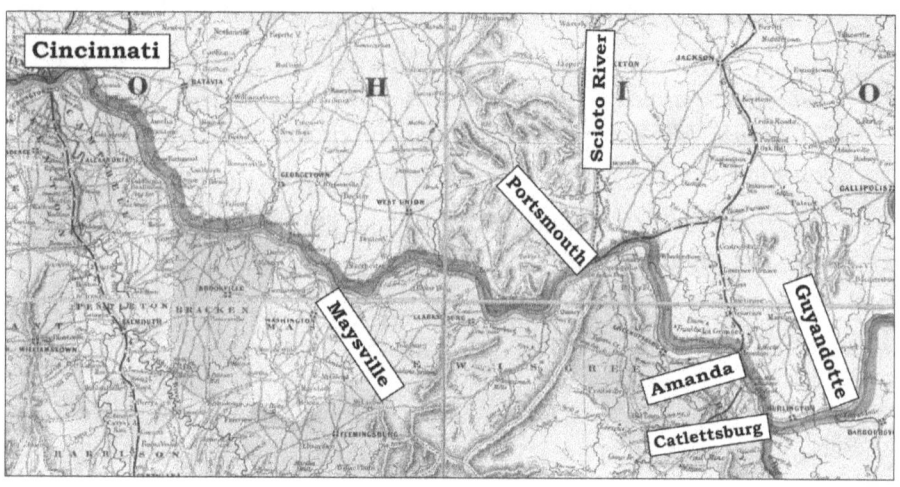

June 28:

Sunrise, passed Maysville, [*Kentucky*], a flourishing place [*the*] size of Madison. Cholera raged very much.

Twelve [*noon*], passed Portsmouth, [*Ohio*], at [*the*] junction [*of the Ohio and*] Scioto River, and termination of [*the Ohio and Erie*] Canal. Portsmouth looks as if a cargo of paint was needed.

Five [*p.m.*], passed Amanda, Kentucky, quite a swell place; has considerable of iron works called Caroline Furnace.

Six, passed Big Sandy River or Creek. At its mouth are a few houses, beautifully situated, called Catlettsburg; derives the name from owner of the property, whom it is said will neither sell nor improve. Big Sandy River separates Virginia [*now West Virginia*] from Kentucky.

[*At*] sunset, stopped on [*the*] Virginia [*now West Virginia*] shore for wood.

Nine [*p.m.*], landed passengers at Guyandotte, [*West Virginia*].

A Traveler's Diary from 1835

After leaving Cincinnati around 6 p.m. the previous day, our traveler's steamboat had made good time, chugging some sixty miles up the Ohio River by sunrise the following morning.

Our traveler described Maysville, Kentucky, off the ship's starboard side, as a "flourishing place." And flourishing it was. The town had been named for pioneer settler John May, who acquired land at this natural harbor about 1786 from a previous settler, who'd established a frontier fort three miles away. The settlement that became Maysville was originally known as Limestone, and frontiersman Daniel Boone briefly operated a trading post and tavern there. Maysville incorporated in 1787.

Maysville in 1821 (Wikipedia).

Like other towns along the Ohio River, Maysville grew prosperous from trade along the river, especially after the advent of steamboats. By the time our traveler arrived, Maysville's population had swelled to more than 3,000 citizens, and it had become one of the most prominent commercial centers in the state, second only to Louisville. In one sign of Maysville's importance, the same year our visited passed by (1835), a turnpike was completed joining Maysville with Lexington, Kentucky some 60 miles to the southwest — the first macadam road in the state.

Dozens of people had died at Maysville of cholera in spring/summer of 1833, two years prior to our traveler's arrival. And as our traveler commented, 1835 brought fresh cases of the dreaded contagion, though the outbreak would prove smaller this time.

In later years, Maysville, Kentucky would become famous as the home of bourbon whiskey — a term some say was coined right there in Maysville, a possible hold-over from when the area was part of Old Bourbon County, Virginia. Local barrels of spirits with the phrase "bourbon whiskey" stamped on the bottom were shipped off from its docks to points south, including New Orleans. Maysville's historic Old Pogue Distillery, dating to 1876, is still in operation.

Portsmouth, Ohio, on the north side of the Ohio and just east of the Scioto River, was the next town our traveler passed. This had once been the site of a Shawnee village. The first permanent white settler arrived in the vicinity about 1796, and the town was platted in 1803.

Portsmouth was indeed the southern terminus of the Ohio and Erie Canal. This led northward to Cleveland and Lake Erie, and paralleled the Scioto at this end. Construction of this four-foot-deep, hand-dug canal began in 1825 and was completed about 1832. Both the canal and future rail lines built in the 1840s and '50s would significantly boost Portsmouth's fortunes, leading it to become a major industrial center and factory town in coming decades. But in 1835, the town could have benefitted from a coat of paint, according to our diarist's tart account.

You won't find Amanda, Kentucky on contemporary maps; today it's known as Russell, a suburb of Ashland, in Greenup County, KY.

Kentucky was a large producer of iron, and multiple iron furnaces operated here. The Caroline or "Old Caroline" Furnace, the cold-blast furnace that our traveler mentions, was built in 1833 by Henry Blake, and operated until 1890. The company also owned a nearby steam furnace.

It's possible, however, that the ironworks our traveler saw from his steamboat was actually the Amanda Furnace, erected beside the river by three brothers about 1829. After the furnace ceased operations in 1861, the site was acquired by John Russell and the "Means and Russell Iron Company." A townsite was laid out in 1869, originally dubbed "Riverview." In 1873, local landowners agreed to rename the town after its founder, Russell.

Catlettsburg, Kentucky, at the mouth of the Big Sandy River, got its name from owner Alexander "Sawny" Catlett, a Virginian who arrived with his family and several slaves in 1798. The Catlett *family built a log structure about 1812, which served as a combination inn, tavern, trading post, and post office. (The building, enlarged over the years, is still standing.)*

After Alexander Catlett died in 1823, his his son, Horatio, took over the business. But soon Horatio found himself in financial difficulty. The property was lost to a mortgage-holder named Wilson, and in 1833, was inherited by James Wilson Fry.

James Fry was a "sickly, irritable man," according to a later historian. Just as our traveler noted, Fry initially refused to either sell the land at the mouth of the Big Sandy or subdivide it into town lots. So it's not surprising that our 1835 traveler spotted only a few houses when he passed. It would be 1849 before Fry (then in need of money) would plat a town and began selling off lots.

It's said that Horatio Catlett, son of the original owner, returned to Catlettsburg in 1847, but became so distraught over the loss of his former home that he died instantly from a severed windpipe.

The final place our traveler mentions this day was Guyandotte, (now a part of Huntington, West Virginia), where passengers left the steamboat. Guyandotte was first settled in 1799. Known as the Savage Grant, the property had been allocated to veterans of the French and Indian War who'd served under Capt. John Savage. The town was organized in 1810, and soon featured an early flour mill. By the early 1830s, a road connected it to the county seat at Barboursville. The town would be considered a "hotbed of secession" during the Civil War, and was burned in 1861 by Union soldiers.

Our traveler failed to mention passing Burlington, Ohio (roughly 11 miles west of Guyandotte/Huntington, and on the opposite side of the river), perhaps because by the time they passed, dusk obscured it from view.

Burlington was the county seat of Lawrence County, Ohio and the town had been platted in 1817. By 1833 the town was still fairly small, with its population of about 200. Even so, it boasted a courthouse and jail, a school, two churches, a steam-driven sawmill, two "carding machines," two stoneware potteries, one tavern, three stores, a blacksmith, tanner, saddler, hatter, two tailors, two cobblers, one silversmith, one brush-maker, a cabinetmaker, one attorney, and one doctor.

A Traveler's Diary from 1835

The Mansion House hotel in Marietta, Ohio was built in 1835, the year our traveler visited. It would be demolished 102 years later. (Inset from 1858 "Map of Washington County, Ohio," by William Lorey (Library of Congress)).

June 29:

Passed little Kanawha River, [*which*] makes on to Virgina.

Half-past five [*p.m.*], touched at Marietta, [*Ohio*], a good slow and sure-looking place, about 1,500 inhabitants.

The Kanawha River, the largest inland waterway in today's West Virginia, is a tributary that flows into the Ohio, stretching roughly 100 miles long. Our traveler would have passed it at Henderson/ Point Pleasant, (West) Virgina.

Marietta, established in 1788, was the first permanent settlement in the Northwest Territory and is the oldest city in what's now Ohio. Its name honored Marie Antoinette, in grateful acknowlegement of France's assistance during the Revolution.

Thanks to its location at the confluence of the Ohio River and the Muskingum, Marietta developed into a ship-building hub, and also prospered thanks to trading in agricultural products from surrounding farms.

The river formed a practical and convenient route for travelers headed north, and early anti-slavery activists established "stations" on the Underground Railroad here for people escaping slavery.

Once again, our traveler provides a good estimate of the town's population, reporting 1,500 inhabitants in 1835. Five years later, the 1840 Census would confirm Marietta to have 1,814 residents.

A Traveler's Diary from 1835

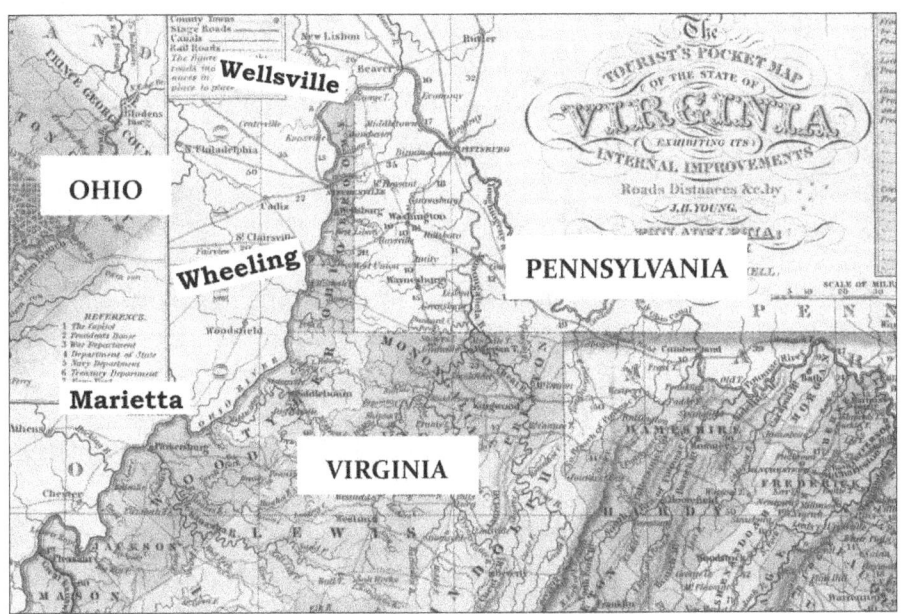

Leaving Marietta, Ohio the previous evening, our traveler continued up the Ohio River, reaching Wheeling (WV) in early morning, and Wellsville (OH) late afternoon. This part of Virginia would split off during the Civil War to become West Virginia. (Portion of 1834 "Map of Virginia," by J.H. Young (LOC)).

June 30:

Six [a.m.], arrived at Wheeling, [West] Virginia. Seven or eight thousand inhabitants, apparently a place of not very much business.

Half-past seven [a.m.], left Wheeling.

Last evening at eight [p.m.], was run [a]foul of by the *Mountaineer*, which done some damage, besides inundating our cabin with ladies, oh dear.

Ten [a.m.], sunk [a] flat load [of] wood, being third sunk on the trip.

Two [p.m.], so very cold, made [a] fire in the cabin. Half past four, touched at Wellsville, [Ohio], quite a smart little place.

After leaving Marietta, our traveler's steamboat continued all through the night, heading northeast up the Ohio River. Ohio was on his left, while Virginia (soon to become West Virginia) was on his right.

Virginia would fracture politically in the coming years, just one example of the painful rending of the fabric of the country during the Civil War. At a convention held in Richmond in April, 1861, the eastern counties of Virginia voted to support secession, while the western counties opposed it. Dissatisfied with the vote, the western counties met twice at Wheeling in the next few months and "reorganized" the state with a competing set of governmental officers. Initially dubbed 'Kanawha,' the new entity was quickly renamed West Virginia.

West Virginia would be admitted to the Union in 1863, on one condition: that the state's constitution provide for the eventual abolishment slavery (which it did; slavery was fully banned in West Virginia in February, 1865).

Our traveler's first stop on this day (for an hour and a half) was at Wheeling, (West) Virginia. Originally the site of a Revolutionary War fort (Fort Henry), Wheeling began attracting settlers in the late 1780s. The townsite was platted in 1793, and incorporated as a town in 1805. It would officially become a city in 1836, the year after our traveler's visit.

With some 7-8,000 inhabitants when our traveler arrived, Wheeling was one of the larger urban centers he had visited. A "Virginia Gazetteer," published in 1835, identified Wheeling as "one of the first manufacturing towns in the western country," fourth in the state by population. As many as 26 steam engines were in operation, including four iron foundries and three steam-powered flour mills. Tradesfolk included 18 blacksmiths and a dozen stone-and-brick masons. There were even four silversmiths in town. In addition to frequent steamboat arrivals, Wheeling was also served by eight daily stage lines. So it's more than a little surprising that our traveler describes Wheeling as a "place of not very much business."

A Traveler's Diary from 1835

A view of Wheeling in 1854, showing steamboats plying the river. (Gleason's Pictorial, 1854, public domain).

True, at the time our traveler visited a majority of the buildings on Wheeling's Main Street were still small, wooden structures. But newspaper reports in the summer of 1835 expressed high expectations for the town's future. A railroad was being planned to connect Wheeling with St. Louis (though the first train wouldn't actually arrive in Wheeling until January 1, 1853). Yet another news story reported an astonishing 17,000 names on one Wheeling hotel register in just one year. It added that an "active spirit of speculation" prevailed in Wheeling real estate, with building lots changing hands at profits of 50% to 100%, while older frame buildings were in the process of being replaced with sturdy brick structures.

Wheeling also boasted a municipal water works by the time our traveler arrived, completed just the previous year (August, 1834). This featured a steam-powered pump that conveyed river water into a 500,000-gallon stone reservoir; from there it was then distributed through the city via cast iron pipes, made by local foundries – a big improvement over the wooden water pipes in use in many other towns.

A slightly later settler, who would first set foot in Wheeling in January, 1837 and later penned a comprehensive town history, recalled Wheeling society in those early days as "quite refined" and "in the old Virginia style." Northerners, however, could receive a cool welcome. "The term 'Yankee' was not by any means considered a very high recommendation of any person coming to Wheeling to better his fortunes," as this settler tartly put it; Yankees were not thought to have a strong work ethic.

Given Wheeling's advantages, why did our traveler consider business to be slow? Well, like other towns in the region, Wheeling had been ravaged in 1832-34 by cholera. So many people died during those years it was said to be hard to find gravediggers to bury the coffins.

But perhaps the best explanation for business doldrums comes again from that early Wheeling town historian. A general depression had settled over much of the nation in late 1833 through 1834, he said, "like a pall over the land." This downturn had been set off by Pres. Andrew Jackson's decision to yank federal deposits from the Bank of the United States, and the bank's tightening of credit in retaliation. And the resulting financial strain had "prostrat[ed] every business in the country." So it wasn't only Wheeling's business that was suffering.

Our traveler mentions the Mountaineer, an "upper cabin" steamboat, colliding with the Caledonia. Collisions between steamboats were not uncommon, and they occasionally proved fatal. In December, 1835, for example, the Lady Franklin would sink on the Ohio River, drowning some 15 to 16 passengers, after a run-in with another steamboat. Luckily for our traveler — and the Steamboat Caledonia — the damage this time was apparently slight.

FOR NEW ORLEANS,
U. S. MAIL.

The fast running upper cabin Steamboat MOUNTAINEER, Fairman, Master, will depart for the above and intermediate ports, on Saturday, the 19th inst., at 10 o'clock, A. M. For freight or passage apply to
J. C. BUCKLES,
nov 17   Steamboat Warehouse.

Ad for the Steamboat Mountaineer from the Courier-Journal (Louisville, Kentucky), November 19, 1836.

A Traveler's Diary from 1835

Sketch of a flat boat plying the river, with its cargo. (Alfred Waud, from Historic New Orleans Collection (Wikimedia, public domain).

The Caledonia, it seems, wreaked her own share of havoc on the river; they'd sunk at least three "flat loads of wood" on this trip alone.

So, what was a "flat load of wood"? We don't know for sure. It could have been a small river craft known as a "flat boat" carrying firewood or milled lumber. As the name implies, these were flat-bottomed cargo boats that used the river's current to carry them downstream. Because the boats had no power, they couldn't make it back up-river on their own. In the early days, these would simply be disassembled and scrapped once they arrived at their final destination (often New Orleans). In later years, they might be towed back upstream by a steamer. Lumber was one of many commodities shipped on flat boats. Cincinnati, with its sawmills, was said to have been "built on the flat boat trade," shipping milled lumber to downstream markets.

More likely, however, the "flat loads of wood" inadvertently sunk by our traveler's steamboat were simply large assemblages of logs, bound together and floating downriver to reach a sawmill or market. Some log rafts were said to reach several acres in size. Larger rafts might even have a hut on top as shelter for a meager crew.

Log rafts were slow, cumbersome, and difficult to steer. And because of their low profile, they were not easily seen, especially at night. As our traveler's experience confirms, collisions between log rafts and steamboats were fairly frequent.

Example of a small log raft, with Wheeling in the background (portion of a view of Wheeling from Gleason's Pictorial, 1854, public domain).

It's hard to believe that a late-June afternoon would have been cold enough to warrant a fire. But our traveler clearly thought so. His mention of building a fire in his cabin confirms his berth was in an upper-class cabin equipped with a central wood stove. This was a luxury that was surprisingly common aboard steamboats. A report about the wreck of The Shepherdess in January, 1844, for example, mentions passengers in the "gentlemen's cabin" sitting around a wood stove just before the ship hit a snag. Interior photos of later steamboats similarly show one or two potbellied stoves for the long communal interior.

That reference to a sex-segregated "gentlemen's cabin" may also explain our traveler's report that the collision with the Mountaineer had "inundat[ed] our cabin with ladies" — presumably refugees from the nearby "ladies' cabin."

Wellsville, Ohio, across the river from the northern tip of (then) Virginia, is thought to have been originally surveyed at the behest of none other than George Washington. Washington and his friend, Col. Willliam Crawford, ventured south by canoe from Philadelphia in 1770, in search of lands to purchase that could be given to former soldiers in the French and Indian Wars. A survey was eventually made about 18 years later, and the surveyor himself bought 30 townships at $6 per <u>100</u> acres. The 304-acre site that would become Wellsville was purchased in 1795 at $6 per <u>one</u> acre.

William Wells, son-in-law of the purchaser and the man for whom the town is named, settled here and founded the town two years later. Although a post office was opened as early as 1816, lots weren't formally subdivided until about 1823.

By 1835, our traveler described Wellsville as "quite a smart little place." Although Columbiana County was primarily an agricultural community, Wellsville itself was a bustling shipping hub, and goods from over a dozen Ohio counties flowed through its port. The town's wonderful harbor was conveniently situated mid-way between Pittsburgh and Wheeling.

The village of Wellsville had been incorporated in 1833, two years before our traveler arrived, and daily stages connected it with Cleveland and Fairport (on Lake Erie). Its business interests would diversify the next year (1836) with the establishment of the Fulton Foundry, opened by Bottenberg & Geisse, which produced equipment for steamboats and, later, brick-making. The foundry would later be owned by Stevenson & Company.

Illustration of the type of heavy equipment produced by Fulton Foundry, from their letterhead (1880s), when the foundry was owned by Stevenson & Co.

A Traveler's Diary from 1835

Pittsburgh, Pennsylvania, as it appeared in the late 1850s (from Ballou's Pictorial, February 21, 1857; WikiMedia Commons, public domain).

July 1:

Seven [a.m.], arrived at Pittsburgh, [Pennsylvania].

At two [p.m.], took Canal Boat *General Lacock* for Allegheny Mountains. The Allegheny and Monongahela Rivers enter into and form the head of the Ohio River at Pittsburgh, from which they have bridges over both streams.

The place [*Pittsburgh*] is built on level ground, completely surrounded by young mountains. They burn coal chiefly, the smoke of which does not rise generally above the hills, which keeps the place completely enveloped most of the time. All the buildings, fences, and every thing about the town are about the color of smith shops generally. Inhabitants not far from 20,000.

Very many steamboats and vessels here, and they have extensive iron works. They are building quite a large stone building intended for [a] county prison.

Paid Steam Boat fare from St. Louis to
Pittsburgh: $ 22.00

Laundry   .75

B[*reakfast*] and D[*inner*] at Pittsburgh: .75   1.50

Pittsburgh was a city of considerable size for 1835. Our traveler estimated roughly 20,000 inhabitants; the 1840 Census would peg the population at 21,115.

As our traveler noted, a stone penitentiary was under construction when he arrived. The first prison completed west of the Atlantic states, this prison was situated north of Pittsbugh proper, embracing some 12 acres within its outer fence. Dubbed the Western Penitentiary, it resembled a medieval castle, complete with turrets.

Early sketch of Western Penitentiary at Pittsburgh, Pennsylvania, circa 1850s. (Public domain).

The original version of this prison had opened in 1826. But within a decade, its 8' x 12' cells were found too small to humanely house the prisoners, who were forced to both live and work in solitary confinement. The initial cells were scrapped and the prison redesigned. Work was in progress on the newly-reconfigured prison when our traveler visited in 1835; it would begin housing prisoners in 1836. During the Civil War, this prison would hold over 100 Confederate prisoners captured during Morgan's Raid.

Interestingly enough, although our traveler had boarded the Steamboat Caledonia at St. Louis back on June 22nd, he didn't actually pay the steamboat's fare until it reached the end of its route at

Pittsburgh (a hefty $22.00, the equivalent of $673 in today's dollars).

At Pittsburgh, our traveler disembarked and took passage on a much smaller canal boat, the General Lacock, to head farther east through the Allegheny mountains.

From here he was embarking on a segment of the Pennsylvania Canal known as the Western Division. The canal had only had been completed through Johnstown (at the base of the mountains) in 1831. The 104-mile Western Division of the canal included 68 locks, 16 dams, and 16 aqueducts. Canal boats were pulled along the waterway by mules from a tow-path that lined the canal.

From Johnstown, an ingenious "portage railroad" over the mountains had opened just the previous year, 1834. This would transport our traveler's canal boat by rail some 37 miles, up and over the uncanal-friendly mountains separating Pittsburgh from Philadelphia. The railroad climbed 1,171 feet from Johnstown, reaching a peak of 2,322 feet at the summit of the Alleghenies. All told, the canal-slash-railway combination now cut the travel time from Pittsburgh to Philadelphia from 23 days to just four. No doubt our traveler would have been excited at this improvement.

The canal boat "General Lacock" that our traveler boarded at Pittsburgh was undoubtedly named after Abner Lacock, a prominent Pennsylvania politician and judge. Among other posts, Lacock had served from 1808-1810 as a member of the Pennsylvania State Senate, and a U.S. Senator from 1813-1819.

In 1807, Lacock had served as a brigadier general with the Pennsylvania Militia. That duty may perhaps have shaped his view of war. In 1819, he became part of a Congressional committee investigating whether President

Portrait of Abner Lacock circa 1805. (Public domain).

Andrew Jackson had exceeded his authority by waging war with the Seminoles.

Lacock's part in challenging Jackson's authority did not win him any affection from the irascible president. In fact, Jackson once reportedly threatened to "cut Lacock's ears off" at the earliest opportunity. Rather than slinking away from Washington after his term expired to avoid confrontation with the President, Lacock "tarried" a bit to give Jackson an opportunity to call him out. But Jackson, it seems, thought better of further hostilities, "permitting" Lacock to leave Washington with his "ears of natural size," as one historian later put it.

In 1825, Lacock was appointed as a Pennsylvania commissioner, charged with surveying routes for state canals and railway lines. This assignment likely explains why a canal boat would have been named for him.

Abner Lacock was still alive in 1835 when our traveler visited Pennsylvania. He was now back in politics, serving as a member of the state's House of Representatives. He would pass away just two years later, in 1837, at the age of 66.

As our traveler stepped aboard the small canal boat this July mid-afternoon, he was probably looking forward to cooler air ahead in the Allegheny Mountains. And perhaps he was looking forward, as well, to returning home – he now was less than a week away from the end of his journey.

A Traveler's Diary from 1835

The Pennsylvania Canal through Saltsburg, circa 1900. (Courtesy of Saltsburg Historical Society).

July 2:

At seven [*a.m.*], passed Kiskiminetas Falls and entered the [*Kiskiminetas*] River, and went two miles [*up-river*] before entering the Canal again. Salt works and coal mines line the margins of this river.

Ten [*a.m*], passed through Saltsburg, (Pennsylvania), about twenty houses, nothing very interesting.

Half past twelve [*noon*], passed through solid rock [*tunnel*], nearly [*a*] quarter mile through, and mountain above 200 feet high.

Half past four [*p.m.*], passed through Blairsville, quite a smart-looking little place, 4 or 5 hundred inhabitants.

This was one of the most interesting segments of our traveler's journey, engineering-wise.

A Traveler's Diary from 1835

From Pittsburgh, the Western Division of the canal first ran northeast. Then it took a jog east following the Kiskiminetas River, a 27-mile-long tributary of the Allegheny River, now colloquially known as the "Kiski." Both salt and coal were abundant in the region, as our traveler noted.

Saltsburg is where the Conemaugh River and Loyalhanna Creek join to form the Kiski. Settlers began arriving at Saltsburg in 1795. Lots were first sold about 1810, and the town was subdivided in 1817. As you might expect, the town drew its name from the local salt industry. Salt was first manufactured nearby in 1812, and by 1813 local wells were producing some 30 bushels of salt a day. By 1833 the town's salt industry had mushroomed, shipping over 4 million pounds of salt downriver that year via the newly-completed Pennsylvania Canal.

Our traveler describes the small settlement in 1835 as about 20 houses, and "nothing very interesting." This likely underestimates the town a bit, as the salt industry at the time he visited was still thriving. Although the salt industry would be largely played-out by 1837, even by 1840, the town would still number 335 souls.

Later descriptions of the canal as it transited Saltsburg offer a fascinating window on just how large an engineering feat this was: some 40 feet wide at the waterline, 28 feet across at the bottom, and four feet deep.

From the canal boat's deck our traveler might have been able to glimpse Saltsburg's small cemetery as he floated by. Begun about 1820, the cemetery lost part of its land to the canal project when the canal was put through in 1829. He may also have caught a brief view of an imposing two-story stone house, built

Home of Saltsburg's first blacksmith, Robert McIlwain, built in 1830 (now the Rebecca B. Hadden Stone House Museum). (Courtesy of Saltsburg Historical Society).

five years earlier in 1830 as a home for Saltsburg's first blacksmith, Robert McIlwain — and still standing today (now a museum).

A bit farther along, our traveler encountered an astonishing and creative engineering marvel. First, an aqueduct carried the canal boat across the entire width of the Conemaugh River in its own raised, artificial channel. From there, the canal boat entered the gloom of an 817-foot-long hard-rock tunnel, just finished in 1830. This was one the few occasions where our traveler seems to have exaggerated just a bit; rather than stretching nearly a quarter-mile in length (1,320 feet), the tunnel was actually less than a sixth of a mile long (880 feet). But perhaps sailing through in darkness made it feel longer!

Blairsville, on the other side of the tunnel, was "a smart-looking place," according to our traveler. He wasn't the only visitor to find the town appealing. Journalist Anne Royall had similarly reported in 1829 that Blairsville "has the appearance of enchantment."

First Presbyterian Church of Blairsville, PA, built 1829. (Public domain).

Like other towns in the region, the area was rich in iron, coal, and salt. Blairsville had gotten its start back in 1788, when James Campbell paid "seven pounds lawful money" to acquire the Lisbon Tract, a large parcel north of the Conemaugh River. By 1818 a few early settlers had arrived. But the area really took off in 1823 after a large toll bridge was constructed over the river by the Huntington, Cambria and Indiana Turnpike Company. This new wagon road happily connected Blairsville with Pittsburgh.

The toll road's massive 300-foot bridge was the largest single-arch bridge in the United States at the time (though sadly, it would collapse in 1874).

With Campbell's land now situated at a major river crossing, he began subdividing his property for a town, naming it after John Blair, president of the Turnpike company that had made such prosperity possible.

The town of Blairsville was formally incorporated in 1825. A sister community named "Brownstown" was launched about the same time by nearby landowner Andrew Brown. This adjacent community would be absorbed into Blairsville in 1890.

Johnstown as it appeared in 1840. What may be a basin where canal boats were moored is just left of the tree trunk. (Courtesy of the Johnstown Flood Museum Archives, Johnstown Area Heritage Association).

July 3:

Arrived at Johnstown, [*Pennsylvania*] at five [*a.m.*], a mean-looking place.

Took Peruvian Line [*canal boat*] for Philadelphia.

Ten [*a.m.*], after ascending three inclined planes, reached summit of Allegheny mountains, eleven hundred feet above Johnstown. The mountaineers look hard [*strong*] and healthy. That said, they can have no other inducement [*for living here*].

Arrived at Hollidaysburg, and took canal boat at one o'clock.

Half past four [*p.m.*], passed Williamsburg, [*Pennsylvania*], a small goodly-looking little place on either side of the canal.

Nine [*p.m.*], passed through Alexandria [*Pennsylvania*], [*which*] looked finely with the mountains lying on its bosom.

A Traveler's Diary from 1835

Johnstown, at the western foot of the Allegheny Mountains, was the eastern terminal of Pennsylvania's Main Line Canal. From here, canal boats heading east were transferred onto railroad cars of the Portage Railroad to make the journey over the mountains (and on the return trip, would be placed back in the canal basin at Johnstown). The Portage Railroad was quite the tourist attraction. Novelist Charles Dickens would pay a visit to Johnstown in 1842 during his own adventure on the canal.

Johnstown had once been the site of an early Indian trading village. First surveyed in 1769, the land originally belonged to the Iroquois tribe. Settler Josef Schantz (also known as Joseph Johns), a Swiss-German emigrant, acquired the 249-acre tract in 1793 for $8.50 an acre. He erected a house the following year, and began clearing land for farming.

Schantz/Johns subdivided a townsite in 1800. It was originally called 'Schantzstadt,' but this soon was replaced by the Americanized version, 'Johnstown.' Level farmland was not abudant nearby, and despite Johns' high hopes, his townsite did not grow as rapidly as he would have liked. After Johnstown was passed over for the honor of Cambria County seat, Johns sold out in 1807 and moved on. But the town he'd launched continued to slowly grow. By 1828 the population had reached 200.

In 1831, Johnstown incorporated itself as Conemaugh Borough, and then renamed itself 'Johnstown' in April, 1834. That same year, the Pennsylvania Canal was finally completed through Johnstown. The town's fortunes were finally looking up.

Although our 1835 traveler called it a "mean-looking place," Johnstown could now boast a church; a newspaper; a distillery, and a drugstore. And, thanks to business brought by the canal, it would continue to grow. By 1850, the town's population would reach 1,259. And in 1856, just six years later, it had skyrocketed to 6,000.

The "Peruvian" canal boat on which our traveler booked passage was piloted by Capt. Coyt. The canal boat, as we've noted, would have been transferred to a rail car at Johnstown. From there, the Portage Railroad carried the boat on to Hollidaysburg, an amazing 37-mile journey over the Allegheny Mountains.

A Traveler's Diary from 1835

One of the ten "inclines" of the Portage Railroad, showing two canal boats on rail cars being hauled up the incline. (Sketch by George W. Storm of the Old Portage Railroad, 1857. Public domain).

The Portage Railroad line featured ten long grades or "inclines," five on either side of the summit. (It's unclear why our traveler noted only three on his ascent). Steam engines at the inclines hauled the rail car up the steep grade. On the flatter sections between inclines, horses or train engines propelled the rail cars along. At the top, a tunnel cut through the last of the mountain. And gravity did the work on the downhill journey.

Wire ropes would be used at the inclines, beginning in 1842. But when our traveler made the journey, the hoisting works would have still been using hemp rope.

All-told, as our traveler mentioned, he rose more than 1,100 feet in elevation aboard the train: from 1,171 feet at Johnstown to 2,322 at the summit. After the rail car descended on the eastern side, the canal boat would have been taken off the railroad and placed back in a large canal basin at Hollidaysburg, Pennsylvania. This man-made pool was huge: 120 feet wide, and six feet deep, and two miles long.

A Traveler's Diary from 1835

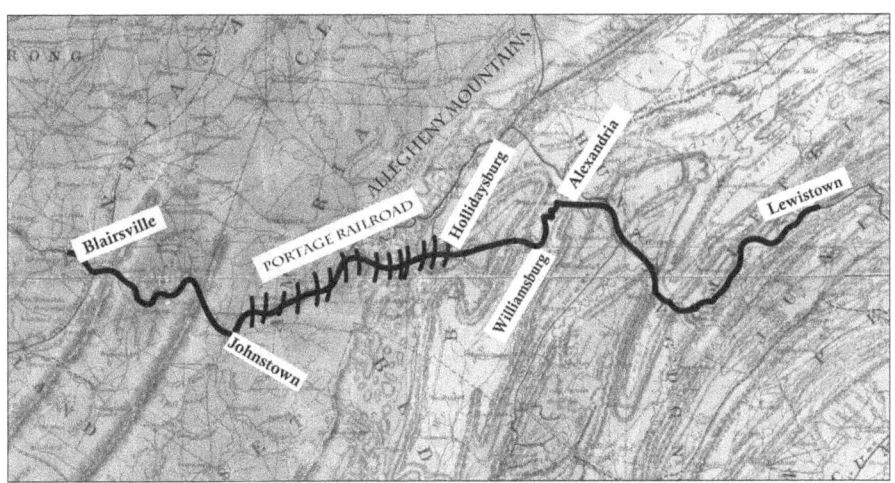

1857 map of Pennsylvania, annotated to show the Pennsylvania Canal and Portage Railroad over the Allegheny Mountains. (1857 map of Pennsylvania by Charles De Silver, Library of Congress).

The boat then would navigate from the basin into the next segment of the Pennsylvania Canal, known as the Juniata Division.

Hollidaysburg had been named after a pair of Irish immigrants, Adam and William Holliday, who'd laid out the townsite in 1796. But for decades, its relatively remote location kept the town small. As late as 1827, the town's population was just 76 people.

By 1835, however, all that had changed. Although our traveler didn't leave behind a single word of description, Hollidaysburg was now undergoing rapid expansion, thanks to completion of the canal the previous year. Luckily, a different visitor that same year did pen a verbal picture, describing Hollidaysburg as "so unfinished that one might suppose it to have been built within a year," but adding: "many substantial buildings are going up, and it is evident that rapid increase is the destiny of the town."

By 1837, Hollidaysburg would boast 14 boat lines making daily stops. At the height of the canal era, a canal boat would arrive every 20 minutes.

One of those "substantial new buildings" erected at Hollidaysburg in 1835 was a large inn for travelers, patriotically dubbed the

'U.S. Hotel.' Although the original structure succumbed to a fire in 1871, the hotel was rebuilt in 1886, and this second incarnation still stands. Two Hollidaysburg homes dating back to the canal era (1847) have also been preserved.

Hollidaysburg would fade in importance after 1854, when the Pennsylvania Railroad's main line was completed. Cheaper, faster rail travel shifted the region's transportation hub to Altoona.

Once a Shawnee and Lenape hunting ground, Williamsburg, Pennsylvania is the oldest borough in Blair County. It was founded in 1790 by Jacob Ake, and later dubbed Williamsburg to honor Jacob's son, William Ake. Perhaps imitating an early design for Philadelphia, Williamsburg was laid out around a central diamond or town square.

By 1820, the Census reported Williamsburg had one inn, one distillery and, sadly, one slave. Like so many towns along the Pennsylvania Canal, completion of the waterway through Williamsburg began spurring growth about 1833.

Williamsburg was described by our traveler as a "goodly-looking place," with buildings lining both sides of the canal. An early charcoal-fired iron works known as Mount Etna Furnace had been established here in 1805, producing pig iron.

Mount Etna Furnace, part of the early iron works at Williamsburg, PA (circa 1968, Library of Congress).

Over time, this operation grew into an extensive complex that included not only a stone furnace but also a grist mill, charcoal house, blacksmith shop, boarding house, 3-family house, two ironmasters' mansions, a paymaster's house, and a store. A Methodist Church was added in 1860, and the cemetery was in use much earlier, with *graves dating back to 1832. The Mount Etna Furnace complex is now preserved as a national historic district.*

After the Pennsylvania Canal was abandoned in 1872, a branch of the Pennsylvania railroad connecting Williamsburg with Hollidaysburg was built along the old canal towpath.

Around 1744, Indian trader John Hart used a hollowed-out log to feed his horses at a site that would eventually become Alexandria, Pennsylvania. Later land claims used Hart's "logg" as a survey or reference point. Even today, the region is known as Hartslog Valley.

The townsite of Alexandria was laid out by Elizabeth Gemmill in 1793, with the street running near John Hart's landmark log named (predictably) "Hartslog Street."

A road connecting Alexandria with Harrisburg, Pennsylvania opened in May, 1808, and Alexandria became the western terminus of the Harrisburg Stage Line. The town was incorporated as a borough in 1827, and the Pennsylvania Canal came through in 1833. By 1840, the town's population had reached 574 people.

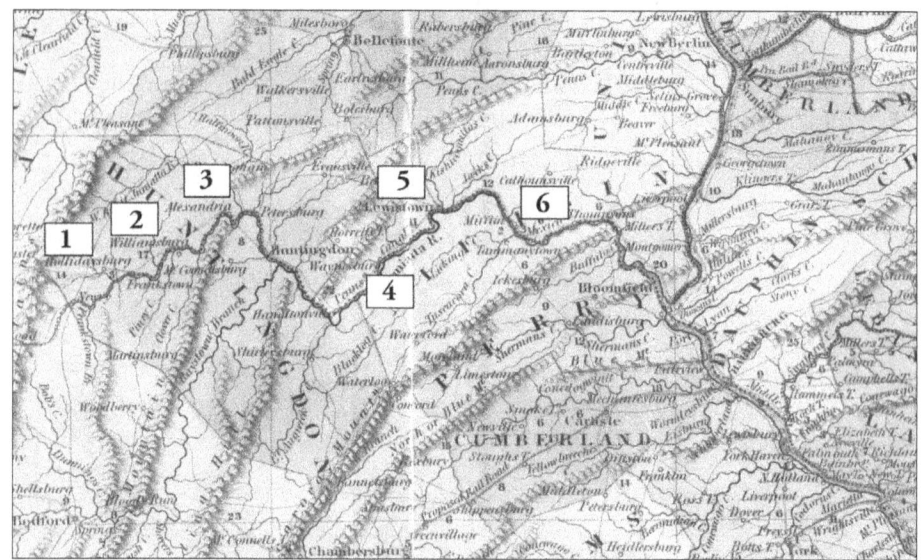

Annotated inset from an 1831 map of Pennsylvania by J.H. Young (Finley's A New General Atlas). Scattered along the Pennsylvania Canal are: (1) Hollidaysburg, (2) Williamsburg, (3) Alexandria, (4) Waynesburg (McVeytown), (5) Lewistown, and (6) Mexico.

July 4:

Disturbed by the steward very early this morning.

The canal [*is*] following the course of the River Juniata.

Quarter before nine [*a.m.*], passed through Waynesburg [*Pennsylvania*], a small place 68 miles from Hollidaysburg.

One [*p.m.*], passed through Lewistown, [*Pennsylvania*], pleasantly situated, but of not much importance.

Five [*p.m.*], relock in Mexico.

The name 'Waynesburg' doesn't appear on modern maps; today, it's McVeytown, in Mifflin County, Pennsylvania. Samuel Holliday was the first permanent settler in the vicinity, setting down roots in 1762 and erecting the first grist mill and saw mill in what would become Mifflin County.

The town of Waynesburg was laid out about 1795, and a post office opened there about 1808. It was incorporated as a borough in April, 1833, and renamed McVeytown. But as you can see by our 1835 traveler's report, the earlier name 'Waynesburg' remained in use for the next few years.

The town's namesake, John McVey, had located a 200-acre tract adjoining Holliday's acreage in 1787, and built himself a log home. Other settlers had soon followed.

By 1800, the settlement of Waynesburg had only a few buildings, including a hotel. Semi-weekly stages soon began serving the town, and a tavern, stores, and blacksmith shop were added. In 1831, a tannery opened. Holliday's early grist mill was abandoned sometime before the canal reached Waynesburg, but he built another mill on the opposite side of Mattawana Creek.

When our traveler arrived, Waynesburg (now officially McVeytown) was still small, but big enough to include a tailor, cabinetmaker, meat market, blacksmith, physician, and several stores.

Slightly farther up the the River Juniata, our traveler passed Lewistown, Pennsylvania. He gave it only a passing glance, dismissing Lewistown in his diary as "pleasantly situated, but of not much importance."

Lewistown's roots already went back three-quarters of a century by the time our traveler saw it. Once a Shawnee village known as 'Ohesson,' the site was settled in 1754 after William Penn's Albany Purchase. Lewistown began as a trading post, built here by Arthur Buchanan and his wife, Dorcas.

The Buchanans weren't there long before hostilities in the French and Indian War prompted them to retreat to Carlisle. Arthur Buchanan died there in 1760, but Dorcas was determined to keep going. In 1765 she returned to the trading post and, with her children, continued to operate it — a most unusual enterprise for a woman. Her trading post is said to have been at the corner of today's South Main and Water Streets, where the Hotel Lewistown now stands.

A Traveler's Diary from 1835

A view of Lewistown, Pennsylvania circa 1860s. (James S. Earle & Sons Stereoview, Library of Congress).

Mifflin County was formed in 1789, and Lewistown became its county seat. Mifflin had been named after Pennsylvania's first governor; Lewistown took its name from William Lewis, a Philadelphia lawyer, judge, and legislator.

Construction of a road to linking Lewistown with Harrisburg prompted more settlers to arrive. And after the Pennsylvania Canal was finished through Lewistown in 1829, the fledgling town began to thrive as a shipping port. Iron ore had also been discovered in the region, and by 1836 some 5 charcoal-driven iron furnaces were in operation.

Completion of the railroad in 1849 drew much of the shipping business away from Lewistown. But the canal continued to operate as late as 1889.

Four hours after passing Lewistown, our traveler "re-locked" at Mexico, Pennsylvania.

The Pennsylvania Canal required more than 100 locks on its Juniata Division stretch alone, lifting or lowering canal boats to account for the varying elevations. Locks were only slightly larger than the canal boats themselves: 15 feet wide and 90 feet long, with a four-foot-wide spillway at the upper end. After a boat entered a lock, large wooden gates would be closed on each end, and hand-operated valves would allow water in or out of the lock to raise or lower the boat inside.

Three locks were required at the "Lewistown Narrows" just below Lewistown: two at the upper end, and one at the lower (likely the lock our traveler mentions at the village of Mexico).

A quarry near Mexico supplied most of the stone used to build the numerous Juniata Division locks. Elsewhere along the Pennsylvania canal, locks were built of dry-laid stone faced with wooden planking or mortared cut stone. But those like the one our traveler mentions at the Narrows were constructed of mortared rubblestone.

Mexico was initially settled in 1751 by Capt. James Patterson, his son William, and several friends, and was known first as "Patterson's Landing." The site held a fort during the French and Indian War (1755-56), then was abandoned in 1756.

A townsite was laid out about 1805 by Tobias Kreider. For reasons that remain unclear, the settlement had initially been dubbed "New Mexico." But by 1812 that was shortened to just "Mexico."

Our traveler made no mention of the town of Mexico itself; just the lock found at the south end of town. Even more than a decade later, in 1847, Mexico was still fairly small: just 30-40 dwellings, three stores, three taverns, a grist mill, sawmill, woolen factory, and two churches.

A Traveler's Diary from 1835

The first Pennsylvania State Capitol building at Harrisburg (from stereoview, Library of Congress).

July 5:

Six in the morning, passed Harrisburg, [*Pennsylvania*], a neat little place, four thousand inhabitants. The State House is located here. It is said to [*have*] cost $300,000; from outward appearance I should think half the amount would pay well for such a building.

Here the canal follows the Susquehanna [*River*]. Passed Middletown, Bainbridge, and Newport.

[At] one [*p.m.*], arrived at Columbia, [*Pennsylvania*], and exchanged [*canal*] boat for railroad car, and started for Philadelphia at four [*p.m.*].

Columbia has about three thousand inhabitants, a place for railroad cars and canal boats; has [*a*] covered bridge across the Susquehanna 1-1/4 mile long.

    Paid fare from Pittsburgh to Columbia $10.00
    Meals by the way   3.25
    Charity &c.   5.00

Half past five [*p.m.*], arrived at Lancaster, [*Pennsylvania*], a clean, neat-looking place, very dutchified in its appearance; about three thousand inhabitants. Took supper and went on our way.

The actual cost of the Harrisburg State Capitol for both building and furnishings was $244,500. Even so, our traveler evidently would have thought the sum was too much.

After passing Harrisburg, Pennsylvania and three other towns on the Susquehanna, he traded his canal boat for a rail car at Columbia, Pennsylvania.

The mile-and-a-quarter-long covered bridge he mentions was the "second" Columbia-Wrightsville bridge, begun in 1832 and completed in July, 1834, just one year before our traveler's visit. Some 5,620 feet in length and 28 feet wide, it was the world's largest covered bridge at the time. This replaced the "first" version of this same bridge, which had been damaged by ice and bad weather in February, 1832.

The railroad line he took was the Philadelphia and Columbia, an 82-mile stretch just completed the previous October. A canal had originally been planned for this route, but when push came to shove, a railroad was deemed both cheaper and more practical.

It's possible that our traveler's rail car was powered by a steam locomotive; but it's also possible that his car was pulled along the track by horses during this early version of the railroad (see ads below). Steam locomotives would soon replace their horse-powered brethren, and by 1836, some 40 steam engines were in use along this line.

The train stopped in Lancaster, Pennsylvania to allow passengers to purchase supper before continuing on toward Philadelphia.

Advertisement for private passenger service along the Philadelphia and Columbia railroad. Lancaster Intelligencer, September 25, 1835.

Competition among private rail carriers was stiff. This horse-drawn line advertised "fare reduced!" Lancaster Intelligencer, July 17, 1835.

A Traveler's Diary from 1835

CHAMBERLIN'S
North American Hotel.

The Cars from Philadelphia on their way to Columbia, stop at 2 o'clock every day, in front of the North American Hotel, for one hour, for the accommodation of the passengers, who wish to dine, or obtain refreshments. Dinner is always on the table at Chamberlin's, when the cars arrive, and every required refreshment furnished on the instant.

June 19   52—tf

Chamberlin's "North American Hotel" at the southeast corner of Chestnut and N. Queen Streets in Lancaster offered meals for rail passengers. It's possible this is where our traveler took his supper. (Lancaster Intelligencer, July 17, 1835).

A Traveler's Diary from 1835

Chestnut Street, Philadelphia, between 2nd and 3rd Streets, ca. 1842 (daguerreotype by William Y. McAllister, Library of Congress).

July 6:

Five in [*the*] morning, arrived at Philadelphia.

Breakfasted at Tremont House; took Steam Boat *Trenton* at ten [*a.m., heading*] for New York.

A Traveler's Diary from 1835

Half-past eleven, touched at Burlington, [*New Jersey*], quite a pretty place, very much ornamented by trees. Opposite is Bristol, [*Pennsylvania*], quite a seaport-looking place.

One [*p.m.*], took the [*rail*] car at Bordentown, [*New Jersey*].

Half past three, [*took*] Steam Boat *Swan* at Amboy [*New Jersey*]. Touched at Elizabethtown, [*New Jersey*].

July 6:

2 pair draw[er]s
Flannel shirts
4 shirts, 8 collars
5 pair stockings
2 handkerchiefs

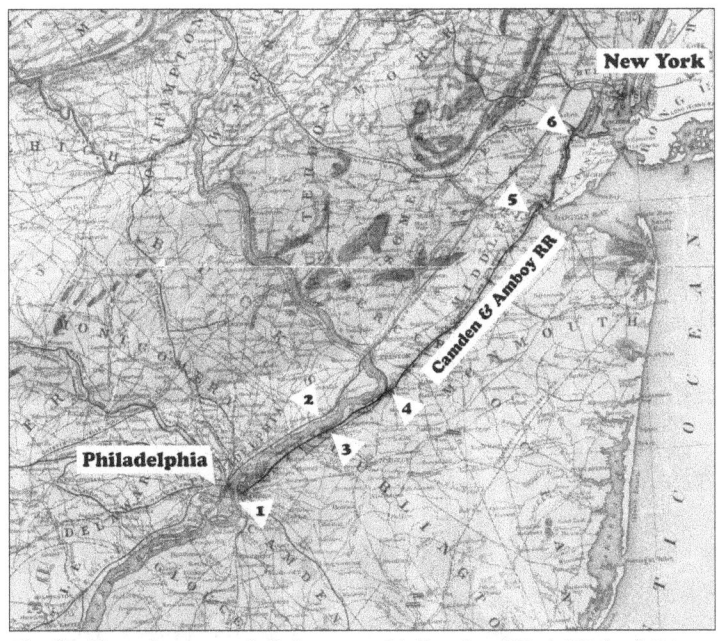

The final leg of our traveler's journey: (1) Camden, NJ; (2) Bristol, PA; (3) Burlington, NJ; (4) Bordentown; (5) Amboy; (6) Elizabethport, and finally New York City. (Geographic and Topographic Map of Pennsylvania and New Jersey, Charles De Silver, 1857)(Library of Congress).

This was our traveler's final day of travel – or at least the last day that he recorded.

The Tremont House, where our traveler ate breakfast in Philadelphia, sat in the busy 100 block of Chestnut Street, across the street from a saddle-maker.

After breakfast he caught the Steamboat Trenton, which he boarded at the foot of Chestnut Street. The Trenton was an early engineering marvel, launched in 1824. Built by R.L. Stevens at Hoboken, New Jersey, this was said to be the fastest steamboat in the world in 1825, reaching a top speed of 12 nautical miles per hour. A sidewheel steamer, she was the first on the Delaware River to feature two smokestacks, and the first with boilers mounted on guards outside her hull.

The Trenton plyed the route between Philadelphia and Bordentown, New Jersey for many years. In 1852, she would carry the coffin of Kentucky statesman Henry Clay (and six accompanying senators) from Philadelphia to New York.

Sadly, the Steamboat Trenton would capsize during a hurricane on September 1, 1879, near Baton Rouge, Louisiana. Although she was righted again and placed back in service, bad luck dogged her thereafter. A ferry collided with the Trenton in December, 1880, damaging her wheelhouse. By December, 1882, she had been relegated to breaking ice on the Delaware River for the Pennsylvania Railroad. Finally, in March, 1884, this once-proud steamboat – now 60 years old – would be sold for just $1,600 to a "junker" to be scrapped.

At Bordentown, New Jersey, our traveler left the Steamboat Trenton behind and boarded the Camden and Amboy Railroad for the short hop to Amboy. Pulling his train would have been the famous "John Bull" engine, shipped in pieces from England in 1831 and assembled (without blueprints) by Isaac Dripps, a young Amboy mechanic. The engine had made a trial run in November, 1831, carrying state legislators and Napoleon's older brother, Joseph Bonaparte. But it had only been placed in service in 1833, two years before our traveler arrived. Today, the John Bull is the oldest surviving locomotive in the nation, and can be seen at the Smithsonian.

At Amboy, our traveler caught another steamboat, the Swan, which made daily runs between Amboy, New Jersey and New York City.

The "John Bull" locomotive (Smith H. Oliver, "The First Quarter-Century of Steam Locomotives in America," Gutenberg Project).

The Swan "touched" briefly at Elizabethtown [Elizabethport], New Jersey on the way, and that's the last place-entry in his diary. But he had booked his passage through to New York. Though his diary ends without further details, New York is almost certainly where he debarked. The last dated diary entry is just a brief list of purchases, and New York City is probably where our traveler did this final round of shopping. Perhaps the excitement and hubub of the big city distracted him, or maybe he simply was no longer worried about economizing. For once, he doesn't record the cost of his purchases for us.

This view across Hudson Bay is similar to what our traveler might have seen as he approached New York: Staten Island (foreground), with Jersey City in the distance on the left, and Brooklyn, New York on the right. (Illustration by Charles W. Burton, ca. 1849, Library of Congress).

A Traveler's Diary from 1835

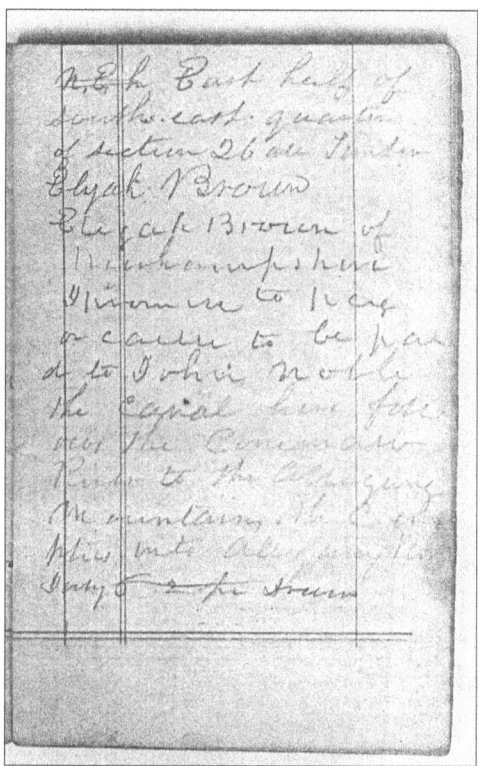

The last entry of our traveler's diary contains a partial legal description and a repeated reference to 'Elijah Brown' of New Hampsire – possibly the name of the writer himself.

Brief notations in back of diary:

East half of [*the*] southeast quarter of Section 26, all timber

Elijah Brown

Elijah Brown of New Hampshire

I promise to pay or cause to be paid to John Noble –

A few tantalizing pages fill the back of the diary, written upside-down to the rest of the entries. These appear to be rough notes, where

A Traveler's Diary from 1835

our diarist evidently composed his thoughts before committing them to paper elsewhere. This also is where his letter of June 14 to Messrs. Robinson appears, though to preserve the chronology I have included the letter with his narrative for that date.

Two brown, brittle newspaper clippings were tucked in the back pages of the diary, one cut from a Newport, Rhode Island newspaper known as "The Mercury" dated about December, 1834, and the other (undated) from the "New York Advocate & Journal." Both are poems. The first is titled "Address of a Child's Departed Spirit, to his Parents." The second poem, "The Departed," includes the sweet sentiment, "If we miss them below, we shall meet them above." Perhaps our traveler had recently lost someone near and dear to him.

Most tantalizing of all, however, are two brief, cryptic mentions of "Elijah Brown" in the very last diary entry. They are part of an incomplete draft for a legal document, suggesting Elijah was about to give a promissory note to purchase timber land from one John Noble.

Was Elijah Brown our diarist? If so, did he make his way back to New Hampshire after stepping off the Steamboat Swan at bustling New York City? Most of all, what would become of Elijah in later years? Perhaps future researchers will someday fill in the rest of our traveler's tale.

For now, I hope this small volume preserves the fascinating 1835 journey of one curious and intrepid traveler as he explored the still-developing regions that were then our "west."

A Traveler's Diary from 1835

...ow are from the pen of a poet of high
...heart which they do not sooth and raise better
...ard one—for they describe with touching
...l beauty the all-absorbing nature of grief for
...d show that excellence may sometimes become so
...nd chastened in the memory of survivors, as to
...stant and strong an aspiration after heaven. This
...of the loved and lost, like a golden chain from the
...hich contains them, seems to meet the grasp of a
...urner, and he is drawn away from damps and pains
...ard to a near union of holy sympathies.—*Conn. Mir.*

THE DEPARTED.

'Tis sweet to believe of the absent we love,
If we miss them below, we shall meet them above.

The departed! the departed!
  They visit us in dreams,
And they glide above our memories,
  Like shadows over streams;—
But where the cheerful lights of home
  In constant lustre burn,
The departed—the departed
  Can never more return!

The good, the brave, the beautiful!
  How dreamless is their sleep,
Where rolls the dirge-like music
  Of the ever-tossing deep,—
Or where the hurrying night winds
  Pale Winter's robes have spread
Above their narrow places,
  In the cities of the dead!

I look around and feel the awe
  Of one who walks alone—
Among the wrecks of former days,
  In mournful ruin strown.
I start to hear the stirring sounds
  Among the cypress trees;
For the voice of the departed
  Is borne upon the breeze.

The solemn voice!—it mingles with
  Each free and careless strain;
I scarce can think Earth's minstrelsy
  Will cheer my heart again;
The melody of Summer waves,
  The thrilling notes of birds,
Can never be so dear to me,
  As their remembered words.

I sometimes dream their pleasant smiles
  Still on me sweetly fall;
Their tones of love I faintly hear,
  My name in sadness call.
I know that they are happy
  With their angel plumage on;
But my heart is very desolate,
  To think that they are gone.

The departed!—the departed!
  They visit us in dreams,
And they glide above our memories
  Like showers over streams;
But, where the cheerful lights of home
  In constant lustre burn,
The departed—the departed
  Can never more return!

SELECTED FOR THE MERCURY.
Address of a Child's departed Spirit, to his Parents.

Kind parents! why those tears?
  And why those bursting sighs?
No weeping here bedims
  Your little ———'s eyes.

The shades of eve you know
  Were hast'ning along,
When my freed spirit left
  To soar the stars among.

Yet long before the night
  Had drawn her veil around,
The home I left below,
  A better had I found.

So rapidly the soul,
  Unbodied, takes its flight,
That scarce earth's scenery fail'd
  When Heaven's broke on my sight.

Did not you, mother, see
  That bright celestial band
That smil'd and beckon'd me,
  And held the inviting hand?

They let me stay a while
  To hear my mother pray;
And see her close the eyes
  And kiss the unconscious clay;

And then to Heaven we flew,
  The cherubs led the way;
But my rapt spirit smil'd
  As joyously as they.

Father! I never knew
  'Twas such a place as this;
That Heaven you told me of
  Was quite so full of bliss.

Oh! there is music here!
  The softest, sweetest strains
Float constantly along
  O'er those ethereal plains.

List, Mother! Father! list!
  A harp to me is given,
And when I touch the strings,
  'Tis heard all over Heaven.

And shall I tell you, who
  Stood ready to embrace
Your little darling one
  In this most glorious place?

'Twas Grand-pa's honor'd name!
  No more with age opprest,
Or toil,—for in this world
  Are youth and endless rest.

Those hoary hairs no more
  Stray o'er his furrow'd brow,
But looks of brightest hue
  Adorn his temples now.

His trembling voice is chang'd?
  The trace of earthly cares
If banish'd from his cheek;
  And God has wip'd his tears.

And, Mary! sister's here;
  She has a cherub's wing,
Can reach their loftiest flights,
  Their noblest anthems sing.

Dear parents! weep no more
  For those you lov'd so well;
For glories here are ours,
  And joys we may not tell.

Oh! live and serve the Lord,
  The dear Redeemer love;
Then, when you've done with earth,
  We'll welcome you above.

The undated clipping on the left likely came from the New York Advocate & Journal, published by Acker, Tindall & Marshall, while the clipping on the right was from the Newport (R.I.) Mercury about December 20, 1834, the year before our traveler's journey.

A Word To Our Readers:

Well, this isn't *really* the end. New puzzle pieces of history have a way of turning up when you least expect them, with fresh bits of information to help complete the picture. If you have additions or corrections for this book, or better yet, new *stories* or images of the places mentioned, please reach out! We'd love to hear. Here's where you can get in touch:

www.Clairitage.com

And if you loved this book (and we sincerely hope you did), kindly share it with your friends!

Here's to History!

For Further Reading

Books:

Chicago City Directory (1844): *http://www.donslist.net/PGH-Lookups/cgi-bin/HandOff-1_0.cgi?Chicago1844+Chicago 1844+000bSP*

Chicago City Directory (Hall Smith, 1853-53): *https://www.familysearch.org/library/books/records (item 510946)*

Dunlop, M.H., Sixty Miles from Contentment: Traveling the 19th Century American Interior (Routledge/Taylor Francis Group, 1995).

Haydon, Roger (ed.), Upstate Travels: British Views of Nineteenth Centuery New York (Syracuse Univ. Press 1982).

Detroit City Directory (1837): *https://www.familysearch.org/library/books/records/item/395792-directory-of-the-city-of-detroit-with-its-environs-and-register-of-michigan-for-the-year-1837-containing-an-epitomised-history-of-detroit-c?offset=11*

Ely, William, The Big Sandy Valley: A History of the People and Country (1887)(describing the founding of Catlettsburg, KY), *available through* Google Books: *https://www.tinyurl.com/44r7xj34*.

Hurt, R. Douglas, The Ohio Frontier: Crucible of the Old Northwest, 1720 - 1830 (Indiana Univ. Press, 1996).

Illinois State Gazetteer: (1858-59) *https://www.yumpu.com/en/document/read/51612821/1858-59-illinois-state-gazetteer-directory-chicago-billiard-museum*

Johnson, Paul, The Birth of the Modern: World Society 1815-1830 (Harper Collins 1991): A fascinating summary of the inventions and institutions that changed the world, including Fulton's patent on the steamboat (1807) and the first telegraph (1838). In 1830, nearly 400 steamboats were plying the Ohio and Mississippi Rivers; and up to the 1940s, nearly a third of Mississippi steamboats would be lost in accidents. Also recites terms for purchasing land at Land Offices in Cincinnati, Marietta, and elsewhere: $2/acre (later $1.25) for 160 acres, 25% down, and four years to pay.

Kilbourn, John, The Ohio Gazetteer (11th Ed., 1833), p. 110: *https://www.tinyurl.com/jk46s3xf* (listing for Burlington, Ohio).

Martin, Joseph, The Virginia Gazetteer (1835): *https://catalog.hathitrust.org/Record/008587590*.

Sheriff, Carol, The Artificial River: The Erie Canal and the Paradox of Progress, 1817 - 1862 (Hill & Wang, 1996).

Whittlesey, Charles, The Early History of Cleveland, Ohio (1867) (*available online: https://babel.hathitrust.org/cgi/pt?id=loc.ark:/13960/t5j96hc0n&view=1up&seq=7*)

Wilde, Joseph L., The "Leader" Wheeling (WV) City Directory, 1879-80: *https://www.familysearch.org/search/catalog/2650159?availability=Logan%20Utah%20FamilySearch%20Library* (Includes a fascinating and very detailed look back at Wheeling in January, 1837, when the writer first arrived in town, describing its Main Street buildings as largely small wooden structures, but society as "quite refined.").

Newspapers (most available from *Newspapers.com*):

Report of a fire in Detroit which swept up as far as the Steamboat Hotel: *Alton (Illinois) Telegraph, May 17, 1837*.

Roger Allen, "Rice Growers Set Up Shop in South Carolina, Georgia" (*Stateboro Herald, December 5, 2014*) (*https://www.statesboroherald.com/local/columnistseditorials/bulloch-history-with-roger-allen-rice-growers-set-up-shop-in-south-carolina-georgia/*)

Mentions of the Steamship *Caledonia*: *Carlisle (PA) Weekly Herald, April 28, 1836* (carrying colonists headed for

Marion City, MO with pre-cut lumber for houses); *U.S. Gazette* (Philadelphia), September 2, 1825 (reflecting her tonnage and passenger capacity; her captain, at the time, was named Buchannan).

Mentions of the Steamship *Mountaineer*: *Montreal Gazette*, August 20, 1833 (describing her as "small, but the accommodations good"); and *Vicksburg Tri-Weekly Sentinel*, October 7, 1839 (mentioning her "light draft.") The Mountaineer had plied the waters of Lake George in the 1820s, before moving south to serve the New Orleans trade in the 1830s. See also *Frankfort (KY) Argus*, December 22, 1837 (reporting that a crew member was wanted for a murder in Kentucky, and the captain wasn't cooperating). Earlier that same year, however, the Mountaineer had helped rescue victims of a steamboat boiler explosion in Ohio. *Vermont Phoenix* (Brattleboro, VT), January 6, 1837. Newspaper advertisements suggest that the steamship's helm changed frequently; her master was Lucius C. Larabee in 1833; Fairman in 1836; James Young in 1837; and G.H. Packard in 1839.

Describing Wheeling, (West) Virginia's prosperity in 1835: *Niles National Register* (St. Louis), May 30, 1835 (mentioning hotel traveler statistics and a "spirit of speculation" in real estate); mention of a possible railroad line from St. Louis to near Wheeling: *Lancaster (PA) Intelligencer*, May 22, 1835.

Steamboat collision: *The Lady Franklin* of Jackson, Mississippi sank on the Ohio River with 15-16 passengers lost, after a collision with another ship: *The Weekly Mississippian* (Jackson, Miss), December 25, 1835.

Steamboat Trenton: Capsized in hurricane near Baton Rouge: *New Orleans Daily Democrat*, September 3, 1879; struck by a ferry: *The Times* (Philadelphia), December 22, 1880; used to break ice on the Delaware River: *Courier-Post* (Camden, NJ), December 21, 1882; sold for scrap (and describing her construction): *Delaware Gazette and State Journal* (Wilmington, Delaware), March 27, 1884.

Magazines/Periodicals:

Serenity Southerland, *Cholera in Detroit: A History* (Michigan Historical Review, Fall 2014): *https://muse.jhu.edu/article/779078/summary*

Catalog of the Exhibits of the Pennsylvania Railroad Company at the World's Columbian Exposition, 1893 (Chicago): *https://www.google.com/books/edition/Catalogue_of_ the_Exhibit_of_the_Pennsylv/jg8aAAAAYAAJ?hl=en &gbpv=1&dq=%22steamboat+trenton%22&pg=PA124-IA3&printsec=frontcover (including mention of Steamboat Trenton).*

Maps/Ephemera:

Map of St. Joseph Co., Michigan *(Home Publishing Co. 1897) - Library of Congress: https://www.loc.gov/resource/ g4113s.la000357/?r=0.259,0.647,0.497,0.292,0*

Map of Branch Co., Michigan *(Geil & Jones 1858) - Library of Congress: https://www.loc.gov/resource/g4113b.la0003 22/?r=0.155,0.486,0.333,0.183,0*

Map of Ohio, Indiana & Michigan *(G.W. Colton 1859) - Library of Congress: https://www.loc.gov/resource/g4071p.rr00 1230/?r=0.371,0.467,0.244,0.143,0*

Bird's Eye View of Coldwater, Branch County, Michigan *(A. Ruger 1868) - Library of Congress: https://www.loc.gov/ item/73693425/*

Map of Cass, Van Buren, & Darrien, Michigan (including Niles) *(Geil, Harley & Siverd, 1860) - https://www.loc.gov/ item/2012593021/*

Map of Pennsylvania *(J.H. Young map, 1831 Finley's 'A New General Atlas'): - mapsofpa.com*

Online Documents & Information:

History of the Erie Canal: *https://eriecanalway.org/application/files/9814/5133/0135/07-2_National_Significance_ Final.pdf*

History of the Canal System of the State of New York, by Noble E. Whitford (Chapter 13: "Slips and Other Adjuncts of the Erie Canal at Buffalo"): *https://www.eriecanal.org/texts/Whitford/1906/Chap13.html*

History of Ashtabula County, Ohio (Conneaut Township) (1878): *http://www.ohiogenealogyexpress.com/ashtabula/ashtaco_1878_hist/ashtaco_1878_hist_pg154_conneauttp.html*

The story of Capt. Chesley Blake: *http://nighttraintodetroit.com/2012/01/20/captain-chelsea-blake-tries-fails-to-avoid-cholera/*

A timeline of Cleveland history: *https://case.edu/ech/timeline*

Commodore Perry's Victory & International Peace Memorial (located on South Bass Island, Ohio): *https://en.wikipedia.org/wiki/Perry%27s_Victory_and_International_Peace_Memorial*

Bill Loomis, "Grand Hotels of Early Detroit" (Detroit News, 2013): *http://blogs.detroitnews.com/history/2013/04/21/grand-hotels-of-early-detroit-cotillions-celebrities-and-turkish-baths/*

Detroit history: *https://nancyford51.wixsite.com/woodward/1800s*

Dane Kelly, "How Michigan Kind Of, Sort Of, Became A State Illegitimately" (The furor over Michigan's statehood): *https://www.clickondetroit.com/all-about-michigan/2019/01/26/how-michigan-kind-of-sort-of-illegitimately-became-a-state-on-jan-26-1837/*

Windsor, Ontario: *https://en.wikipedia.org/wiki/Windsor,_Ontario*

National Register documentation for Detroit Financial District (including historical background): *https://www.nps.gov/nr/feature/weekly_features/2009/DetroitFinancial.pdf*

History of Ypsilanti: *https://cityofypsilanti.com/325/Ypsilanti-History*

History of the Chicago Road: *http://www.michmarkers.com/default?page=S0162*

History of Branch County, Michigan (Everts & Abbott, Phila. 1879): *https://quod.lib.umich.edu/m/micounty/bad0864.0001.001/9?view=image&size=100;* see similarly *https://commons.wikimedia.org/wiki/File:History_of_Branch_county,_Michigan,_with_illustrations_and_biographical_sketches_of_some_of_its_prominent_men_and_pioneers_(1879)_(14777536634).jpg*

Timeline of Coldwater, Michigan: *https://www.coldwater.org/DocumentCenter/View/133/City-of-Coldwater-Historic-Dates-PDF*

History of Coldwater Township, Branch County, Michigan: *http://genealogytrails.com/mich/branch/coldwatertwp.html*

Removal of the Potawatomi Tribe, 1830-1840: *https://en.wikipedia.org/wiki/Potawatomi;* see also *https://www.fcpotawatomi.com/culture-and-history/timeline-of-potawatomi-history/; https://www.pokagonband-nsn.gov/our-culture/history; and potawatomiheritage.com.*

History of the Illinois & Michigan Canal: *https://www.cyberdriveillinois.com/departments/archives/teaching_packages/I_and_M_canal/home.html*

William D. Walters Jr., "Selling Locations - Illinois Town Advertisements 1835-1837" (2010) - *https://geo.illinoisstate.edu/downloads/walters_towns.pdf*

The History of Ft. Beggs in Walkers' Grove (Plainfield), Illinois: *https://drloihjournal.blogspot.com/2018/09/fort-beggs-in-plainfield-illinois-was-a-fort-used-for-one-week-in-may-during-1832-black-hawk-war.html*

Information on the history of Holderman's Grove, *see http:// genealogytrails.com/ill/kendall/history_pioneers.html; see also map: http://www.historicmapworks.com/Map/ US/1593240/Big+Grove+Township++Newark++Lisbon/ Kendall+County+1870/Illinois/*

National Register nomination for Plainfield, Illinois Halfway House: *https://legistarweb-production.s3.amazonaws. com/uploads/attachment/pdf/179298/Nomination_for_ Individual_Landmark_for_24038_W._Main_Street.pdf*

Abraham Holderman's burial site: *https://www.findagrave. com/memorial/12773742/abram-holderman*

The John Hossack home (The Columns) in Ottawa, Illinois: *http://www.johnhossack.com/columns.htm*. The house became a stop on the Underground Railroad. For a fascinating look at the trial of John Hossack for harboring a fugitive slave in 1859, *see https://www.loc.gov/item/ ltf96001561/*

History of Ottawa and the short-lived Fort Ottawa: *https:// www.billwalshchevy.com/history-of-ottawa--il.htm; https://www.britannica.com/place/Ottawa-Illinois;* and *http://www.fortwiki.com/Fort_Johnson_(7)*

Treaty With the Cherokee in 1835 (New Echota): *https://americanindian.si.edu/static/nationtonation/pdf/Treaty-of-New-Echota-1835.pdf; see also https://en.wikipedia.org/wiki/Treaty_of_New_Echota*

History of La Salle County, Illinois (1877): *http://livinghistoryofillinois.com/pdf_files/History%20of%20La%20Salle%20 County,%20Illinois,%201877.pdf*

Henry Schoolcraft, "The Legend of Starved Rock" (1825): *https://cdn.citl.illinois.edu/courses/aiiopcmpss/ StarvedRock/schoolcraft.htm*

Hennepin, Illinois: *https://en.wikipedia.org/wiki/Hennepin,_ Illinois*

Peoria, Illinois: *https://en.wikipedia.org/wiki/History_of_Peoria,_Illinois; see also https://www.peoria.com/commu-*

nity/history.php; map of Peoria: https://www.loc.gov/item/2013593079/; https://collections.carli.illinois.edu/digital/collection/bra_peoria; and http://www.peoriacountyillinois.info/maps.html

The Flanagan House, oldest home still standing in Peoria (story by Molly Crusen): *https://www.peorian.com/history/history-news/local-history/2295-molly-flanagan*

Steamboat Passage, Fares, and disasters - Mid-1800s (John Bowman): *https://steamboat-birthplace-wheeling.com/index.php/2019/06/19/steamboat-passage-and-fare-mid-1800s-by-john-bowman/;* and for a description of various steamboat disasters, by year: *http://genealogytrails.com/ark/greene/SteamboatDisasters.htm*

History of Tremont, Illinois: *http://genealogytrails.com/ill/tazewell/historyoftremont_bios.html*

History of Pekin (Tazewell County), Illinois: *https://www.tcghs.org/photo0101.htm; see also https://fromthehistoryroom.wordpress.com/tag/ann-eliza-cromwell/*

Illustrated Atlas Map of Cass County, Illinois (including Beardstown)*(1874): https://www.loc.gov/resource/g4103cm.gla00038/?st=gallery*

History of Beardstown, Illinois: *http://www.museum.state.il.us/RiverWeb/harvesting/history/settlement/beardstown.html; for story about flooding in 1858, see http://genealogytrails.com/ill/cass/flood_of_1858_at_beardstown.htm*

"Plague on the Prairie: The Cholera Epidemic of 1833 and its Impact on One Illinois Town (Jacksonville, Ill.)," by Greg Olson - *https://www.lib.niu.edu/2002/ih020106.html. For story reporting New Yorkers fleeing town in 1832 to escape cholera, see* Robert McNamara, "The Cholera Epidemic of 1832," *https://www.thoughtco.com/the-cholera-epidemic-1773767.*

History of Meredosia, Illinois: "Harvesting the River" (Illinois State Museum): *http://www.museum.state.il.us/RiverWeb/harvesting/history/settlement/meredosia.html; see also https://morgan.illinoisgenweb.org/township/old-towns.htm*

History of Scott County, Illinois (Naples): *https://sites.rootsweb.com/~ilmaga/scott/scottplat/history.html*

History of Carondelet, Missouri: *https://www.carondeletliving. com/history-of-carondelet*

Quarantine Island and Arsenal Island: *http://usctchronicle. blogspot.com/2013/12/in-search-of-quarentine-island. html*

Smithland, Kentucky history: *http://wkygenealogy.blogspot. com/2010/01/smithland-kentucky-in-1835.html; see also* Historic Sites in Livingston County, Kentucky (Smithland): *https://kentuckylakegateway.com/historic-places/*

Shawneetown, Illinois history: *https://www.britannica.com/ place/Shawneetown; see also https://jg-tc.com/lifestyles/ usas-yesterdays-old-shawneetown-an-important-early-illinois-metropolis/article_33f5ba9c-5cb0-5508-b06a-2e8628202a9b.html.*

Confederate activity in Hawesville: *https://en.wikipedia.org/ wiki/Kentucky_in_the_American_Civil_War; https:// en.wikipedia.org/wiki/Richard_Hawes.*

Economic & Industrial Survey of Cloverport, KY (1952): *https:// digitalcommons.wku.edu/cgi/viewcontent.cgi?article=10 00&context=breckinridge_cty*

History of Cincinnati, Ohio: *https://en.wikipedia.org/wiki/ History_of_Cincinnati; regarding delivery of "air mail" by balloon: https://handeaux.tumblr.com/ post/126502259072/back-in-1835-when-balloonists-were-rock-stars; and see https://www.cincinnatimagazine.com/citywiseblog/artifact-hot-air-balloon-history/; and https://www.wcpo.com/news/insider/history-richard-clayton-balloon*

Maysville, Kentucky - Regarding cholera deaths in 1833: *https://sites.rootsweb.com/~kypendle/Pages/cholera.htm; and see https://kentuckykindredgenealogy. com/2019/09/20/1833-cholera-epidemic-deaths-in-newspapers-a-few-of-the-many/; and regarding both 1833 and 1835 outbreaks: https://www.theaquilareport.com/perspective-the-dreaded-cholera-in-kentucky-1832-1833/; and for its connection to the bourbon industry, see: https://www.cityofmaysville.com/the-b-line/*

History of Portsmouth, Ohio: *https://ohiohistorycentral. org/w/Portsmouth,_Ohio; https://en.wikipedia.org/*

wiki/Portsmouth,_Ohio; regarding the Ohio and Erie Canal: https://www.ohioanderiecanalway.com/learn/canalway-history/historical-timeline/ and https://ohiohistorycentral.org/w/Ohio_and_Erie_Canal

Amanda, Kentucky and the iron furnace: http://www.oldindustry.org/KY_HTML/Ky_No-visit.html; and https://translate.google.com/translate?hl=en&sl=es&u=https://wikies.wiki/wiki/en/Russell,_Kentucky&prev=search&pto=aue; confirming that the Amanda and Caroline furnaces were distinct: https://www.google.com/books/edition/Report_of_the_Geological_Survey_of_Kentu/fjcAAAAQAAJ?hl=en&gbpv=1&dq=Amanda+furnace+Kentucky&pg=PA408&printsec=frontcover; description of the Amanda Furnace as beside the river: https://www.google.com/books/edition/The_Iron_Manufacturer_s_Guide_to_the_Fur/NSJDAAAAIAAJ?hl=en&gbpv=1&dq=Amanda+furnace+Kentucky+steam&pg=PA715&printsec=frontcover. Regarding the Caroline Furnace, see https://www.google.com/books/edition/REPORT_OF_THE_GEOLOGICAL_SURVEY_IN_KENTU/oDY7oENHznQC?hl=en&gbpv=1&dq=Caroline+furnace+Kentucky+steam&pg=PA191&printsec=frontcover

Catlettsburg, Kentucky: https://en.wikipedia.org/wiki/Catlett_House_(Catlettsburg,_Kentucky)

Guyandotte, West Virginia: http://www.wvculture.org/history/journal_wvh/wvh54-2.html

History of Marietta, Ohio: https://mariettaohio.org/about-marietta/history/; for the history of the Mansion House Hotel, see: https://clutchmov.com/mariettas-lost-buildings-lafayette-corner/

History of Wheeling, West Virginia: https://en.wikipedia.org/wiki/Wheeling,_West_Virginia; regarding the Wheeling Water Works in 1834: https://www.ohiocountylibrary.org/wheeling-history/4043; for cholera epidemic in 1832: History of Wheeling City and Ohio County, West Virginia (Gibson L. Cranmer, ed., 1902), https://tinyurl.com/576j7ppu.

The Bank War (Jackson's removal of federal funds): https://www.ushistory.org/us/24d.asp

A Traveler's Diary from 1835

History of Wellsville, Ohio (Frank L. Wells): *http://history.raysplace.com/oh/col-wellsville.htm*

Biography of "General" Abner Lacock (Pennsylvania): *https://www.legis.state.pa.us/cfdocs/legis/BiosHistory/MemBio.cfm?ID=4897&body=S*

History of the Western Penetentiary at Pittsburgh, PA: *http://www.oldwesternpa.com/2016/04/western-state-penitentiary-brief-history.html*

Pennsylvania Canal system and the portage railway over the Allegheny Mountains: Pennsylvania Canal system: *https://en.wikipedia.org/wiki/Pennsylvania_Canal*; about the Western Division of that canal : *https://en.wikipedia.org/wiki/Main_Line_of_Public_Works#Western_Division_Canal*; and for History of the Allegheny Portage Railroad, which carried canal boats over the mountains: *http://www.funimag.com/funimag28/Allegheny01.htm*; and the amazing tunnel, including the only known photo of the aqueduct/tunnel: *https://ourtransportheritage.com/index.php/2020/02/27/a-tale-of-four-tunnels/*

Blairsville (PA) history: *www.blairsvillehistoric.com*; and for the history of the early toll bridge, *see www.historicbridges.org/bridges/browser/?bridgebrowser=pennsylvania/blairsville/*

Johnstown and Portage Railroad history: https://www.jaha.org/edu/discovery_center/work/industry01.html; and see *https://www.wikiwand.com/en/Allegheny_Portage_Railroad. Mention of the 'Peruvian' Line at Johnstown (operated by Capt. Coyt): Pittsburgh Gazette, May 15, 1835.*

Hollidaysburg's *history: https://www.nps.gov/alpo/learn/historyculture/hburgbasin.htm*; some of the town's houses from the canal era still stand: *https://pahistoricpreservation.com/hollidaysburgs-canal-era-houses/*; about the U.S. Hotel, *see: theushotel.com/history.html.*

Williamsburg (PA) history: Information on the Mount Etna Iron Works: *https://en.wikipedia.org/wiki/Etna_Furnace_(Williamsburg,_Pennsylvania)*

History of Waynesburg (McVeytown), PA: *http://www.pagenweb.org/~mifflin/ellis/ellis-10.htm*

History of Lewistown, PA (including "founding mother" Dorcas Buchanan): *https://www.lewistownsentinel.com/news/local-news/2020/04/lewistowns-roots-in-founding-mother/;* for locations of historic buildings/sites, see *https://jrvvisitors.com/wp-content/uploads/2020/03/Walk-Around-Historic-Lewistown-Brochure.pdf*

"Canal in the Mountains" by Scott D. Heberling (Pennsylvania Dept. of Transportation, 2008)*(extensive description of the Juniata Division of the Pennsylvania Canal, and the locks at Juniata Narrows, 10 miles from Lewistown, PA): https://tinyurl.com/a6w54857.*

History of Juniata County, PA (transcription of 1847 I. Daniel Rupp History): *http://genealogytrails.com/penn/juniata/history/1847rupp.html*

Columbia, PA Covered Bridge: *https://www.lancasterhistory.org/finding-aids/columbia-bridge-company-collection-1809-1843/*

Philadelphia and Columbia Railroad: *https://explorepahistory.com/hmarker.php?markerId=1-A-1C0*

Joseph Bonapart, Napoleon's older brother and former king of Spain, owned an 1,800-acre estate at Bordentown, New Jersey at the time our traveler visited, known as "Point Breeze." A portion of this estate recently made national news. Some 55 acres of this original estate will be preserved for public use, with some 50 acres to be a state park. *https://www.inquirer.com/life/bonaparte-philadelphia-bordentown-new-jersey-estate-preserved-20210122.html*

History of the Camden & Amboy Railroad *(including the "John Bull" engine): https://www.jcrhs.org/camden&amboy.html;* see also *https://www.communitynews.org/towns/bordentown-current/residents-rally-to-preserve-historic-bordentown-city-bridge/article_45190c22-adf3-51e9-8258-982b49e312a6.html (effort to save 1831 C&A Railroad bridge at Bordentown).*

Philo E. Thompson would make the same New York/Philadelphia journey as our traveler in 1836 (though in reverse), and similarly mentions not only the Steamboats Trenton and Swan but also Amboy and Bordentown. For Thompson's diary, *see https://journals.psu.edu/phj/article/download/23094/22863).*

Larry Gara, "Yankee Land Agent in Illinois" *(J. Ill. St. Histor. SocSoc., Vol. 44 No. 2 (Summer, 1951)), https://www. jstor.org/stable/40189132 (a fascinating look at a land speculation group of 43 New England capitalists, formed this same summer of 1835).*

LOCAL HISTORICAL SOCIETIES/MUSEUMS:

ILLINOIS:

Alton, Illinois:
Alton Museum of History and Art
Loomis Hall
2809 College Ave
Alton IL 62002
Phone: (618) 462-2763
Website: *www.altonmuseum.com*
Email: *altonmuseum@gmail.com*
Facebook: *@amhainc*

Beardstown, Illinois:
Cass County Historical & Genealogical Society
109 S. Front Street
Virginia IL 62691
Phone: 217-452-7977
Website: *https://www.casschgs.org/*
Email: *cchgs@casscomm.com*
Facebook: *facebook.com/groups/102475096472983/*

Chicago, Illinois:
Chicago Historical Society – Chicago History Museum
1601 N. Clark St.
Chicago IL 60614
Phone: (312) 642-4600
Website: *www.chicagohistory.org*
Email: *research@chicagohistory.org* (Lesley Martin, Research Librarian) *or use form on website*
Facebook: *@chicagohistory*

Hennepin, Illinois:
Putnam County Historical Society
P.O. Box 74, 327 Old Highway 26
Hennepin, IL 61327
Phone: (815) 925- 7560
Website: *http://www.putnamcountyhistoricalsociety.org/*
Email: *pchs61327@yahoo.com*
Facebook: *@PutnamCoHistoricalSoc*

Holderman's Grove, Illinois:
Kendall County Historical Society
7935 Illinois Route 71
Yorkville IL 60560
Phone: (630) 553-6777
Website: *lyonfarmkchs.org*
Email: *lyonfarmkchs1@gmail.com*
Facebook: *@LyonFarmKCHS*

Meredosia, Illinois:
Historical Society of Meredosia Illinois
P.O. Box 304, 305 Main Street
Meredosia IL 62665
Phone: (313) 910-8830
Website: *http://www.museumsusa.org/museums/ info/13981*
Email: *meredosiahistoricalsociety@gmail.com*
Facebook: *@Meredosia-Historical-Society*

Naples, Illinois:
Scott County Historical Society
P.O. Box 85
Winchester IL 62694
Phone: (217) 742-5575

Old School Museum
110 E. Cherry St.
Winchester IL 62694
Phone: (217) 742-8090
Website: *www.OldSchoolMuseum.org*
Email: *oldschoolmuseum@gmail.com*
Facebook: *@OldSchoolMuseumIL*

Ottawa, Illinois:
See **LaSalle County Historical Society/Museum**, under "Utica, Illinois," below.

Pekin, Illinois:
Tazewell County Genealogical and Historical Society
P.O. Box 312
Pekin, Illinois 61555-0312
Phone: (309) 477-3044
Website: *https://tcghs.org/*
Facebook: *@TazewellCountyGenealogicalAndHistoricalSociety*

Peoria, Illinois:
Peoria Historical Society
611 SW Washington St. #A
Peoria IL 61602
Phone: (309) 674-1921
Website: *PeoriaHistoricalSociety.org*
Facebook: *@PeoriaHistoricalSociety*

Plainfield, Illinois:
Plainfield Historical Society/Main Street Museum
23836 W. Main St.
Plainfield IL 60544
Phone: (815) 436-4073
Email: *plainfieldhistoricalsociety.il@gmail.com*
Facebook: *@plainfieldhistoricalsociety*

Shawneetown, Illinois:
Gallatin County Historical Society
c/o John Marshall Museum
434 S. Main St.
Old Shawneetown IL 62984
Phone: (618) 269-3531
Website: *https://gallatincountyhistoricalsociety.webs.com/*
Email: *gallatinhistoricalsociety1818@gmail.com*
Facebook: *facebook.com/Gallatin-County-Historical-Society-305487633725597/*

Tremont, Illinois:
The Tremont Museum and Historical Society
367 South Sampson St., P.O. Box 738

Tremont Illinois 61568
Phone: (309) 840-0094
https://www.tremontil.com/organizations/historicalsociety/index.html
Curator: Lori Fuoss: (309) 925-3827; Email: *lfuoss@telstar-online.net*
Facebook: *@tremontmuseum*

Utica, Illinois:
La Salle County Historical Society/Museum
101 E. Canal St
North Utica IL 61373
Phone: (815) 667-4861
Website: *https://www.lasallecountyhistoricalsociety.org/*
Email: *office@lasallecountyhistoricalsociety.org*
Facebook: *@lchsmuseum*

INDIANA:

Madison, Indiana:
Jefferson County Historical Society History Center
615 W. First St.
Madison IN 47250
Phone: (812) 265-2335
Website: *https://www.jchshc.org*
Email: *research@jchshc.org* or *info@jchshc.org*
Facebook: *@jchshc*

New Albany, Indiana:
Floyd County Historical Society
P.O. Box 455
New Albany IN 47151
Phone: President: David Barksdale: (502) 751-9686
Website: *fchsin.org*
Email: *via website*

Troy, Indiana:
Perry County Museum
P.O. Box 36
125 S. 7th St.
Cannelton IN 47520
Phone: (812) 548-6781 (leave message)

Website: *www.perrycountymuseum.org*
Email: *perrycountymuseum@gmail.com*
Facebook: *@PC Museum*

Utica, Indiana:
Utica Preservation Assn.
106 N. 4th St.
Utica IN 47130
Phone: (812) 288-5110
Website: *www.uticapreservation.com*
Email: *info@uticapreservation.com*
Facebook: *www.facebook.com/pages/Utica%20Preservation/116182341852313/*

KENTUCKY:

Amanda (Caroline Furnace), KY:
Greenup County Genealogy & Historical Society
Greenup Co. Public Library
508 Main Street
Greenup KY 41144
Website: *http://greenupgenealogy.org/greenup_county_genealogy_society_calendar*
Email: *greenupgenealogy@gmail.com*

Carrollton, KY:
Port William Historical Society
1010 Winslow St.
Carrollton KY 41008
Website: *http://www.kykinfolk.com/carroll/portwmhistorical.htm*
Email: *portwilliamhistoricalsociety@gmail.com*
Facebook: *@MastersonHouse*

Catlettsburg, (Boyd County), KY:
Boyd County Public Library - Genealogy Supervisor
1740 Central Avenue
Ashland, KY 41101
Facebook: (*Boyd County KY Genealogy & Family History Research*): *@groups/116682955094479/*

Cloverport, KY:
Cloverport Museum
410 E. Houston St.
Cloverport KY 40111
Phone: (270) 314-3630
Website: *www.gluseum.com/US/Cloverport/150914004979078/The-Cloverport-Museum*
Email: *fawcettcreek@earthlink.net*
Facebook: *@The-Cloverport-Museum-150914004979078/*

Covington, KY:
Kenton County Historical Society
P.O. Box 641
Covington KY 41012
Phone: (859) 491-4003
Website: *https://kentoncountyhistoricalsociety.org/*
Email: *via website*
Facebook: *www.facebook.com/groups/78149103642*

Hawesville, KY
Hancock County Historical Society
Box 605
Hawesville KY 42348

Genealogical Society of Hancock County
P.O. Box 667
Hawesville KY 42348
Phone: (270) 927-8095
(quarterly publication: "Forgotten Pathways')

Hancock County Museum
110 River St.
Hawesville KY 42348
Phone: (270) 927-8672
Facebook: *https://www.facebook.com/pages/Hancock%20County%20Museum/108164525891996/*

Kentucky Historical Society
100 W. Broadway
Frankfort KY 40601
Phone: 877-444-7867
Website: *https://history.ky.gov/*

Email: Andrew Washburn, Curator: *andrew.washburn@ky.gov*

Kyowva Genealogy and Historical Society (a tri-state KY, OH, WV group)
901 Jefferson Ave.
P.O. Box 1254
Huntington WV 25704
Email: *kyowvagen@yahoo.com*
Facebook: *@KyovaGenealogicalAndHistoricalSociety/*

Louisville, KY:
Filson Historical Society
1310 S. Third Street
Louisville KY 40208
Phone: (502) 635-5083
Website: *filsonhistorical.org*
Email: *Research@filsonhistorical.org;* or Librarian (Kathryn Bratcher): *bratcher@filsonhistorical.org*
Facebook: *@TheFilsonHS*

Maysville, KY:
Mason County Historical Society
319 West Third St.
Maysville KY 41056
Phone: (506) 564-0090

Kentucky Gateway Museum Center
(formerly **Mason County Museum**)
215 Sutton Street
Maysville KY 41056
Phone: (606) 564-5865
Website: *https://www.kygmc.org/*
Email: *Sue Ellen Grannis, curator@kygmc.org*
Facebook: *@kygmc*

Milton, KY:
Trimble County Historical Society
P.O. Box 136
Bedford KY 40006
Website: *trimblehistoricalsocietyky.jimdofree.com*
Email: *trimblehistoryinfo@gmail.com*

Facebook: https://www.facebook.com/
groups/234902370315243/about

Newport, KY:
Campbell County Historical & Genealogical Society
8352 E. Main St., 2nd Floor
Alexandria KY 41001
Phone: (859) 491-4003
Website: *https://cchgsky.org/*
Email: *campbellhgs@gmail.com*
Facebook: *facebook.com/campbellcountyhistory*

Paducah, KY:
McCracken County Genealogical & Historical Society
P.O. Box 7651
Paducah KY 42002
Phone: (McCracken Co. Public Library): (270) 442-2510
Website: *https://www.mclib.net/docs/MCGHS.pdf*
Email: *specialcol@mclib.net*
Facebook *(McCracken Co. Area History group): facebook. com/groups/123424704981393*

Smithland, KY:
Livingston Co. Historical & Genealogical Society
117 State St.
P.O. Box 138
Smithland KY 42081
Phone: (270) 928-4656
Website: *www.westernkyhistory.org/livingston/livgensoc.html*
Email: *livingstonhistorical@windstream.net*
Facebook: *facebook.com/groups/414272182881036*

Westport, KY:
Oldham County Historical Society
(Oldham County History Center)
106 N. 2nd Street
La Grange KY 40031
Phone: (502) 222-0826
Website: *http://www.OldhamKYHistory.com/*
Email: *info@OldhamKYHistory.com*
Facebook: *@OldhamKYHistory*

MICHIGAN:

Adamsville, MI:
Cass County Historical Commission
Website: *www.casscountymi.org/HistoricalCommission*
Facebook: *@casscountyhistoricalcommission*

Coldwater, MI:
Branch County Historical Society
27 S. Jefferson St.
Coldwater MI 49036
Phone: (269) 251-7178 (Penny) or (517) 278-2871 (to leave a message)
Website: *https://branchcountyhistoricalsociety.org*
Email: *info@branchcountyhistoricalsociety.org*
Facebook: *@Branch-County-Historical-Society-606732912810574/*

Detroit Historical Society
5401 Woodward Ave.
Detroit MI 48202
Phone: (313) 833-1805
Website: *https://detroithistorical.org*
Email: *jeremyd@detroithistorical.org (Jeremy Dimick, dir. of collections/curator) or museumstore@detroithistorical.org*
Facebook: *@DetroitHistoricalSociety*

Niles, MI:
Niles History Center
508 E. Main St.
Niles MI 49120
Phone: (269) 845-4054
Website: *www.michigan.org/property/niles-history-center*
Email: *NilesHistory@nilesmi.org*
Facebook: *@NilesHistoryCenter*

St. Joseph, MI:
Berrien County Historical Society
313 Cass St., P.O. Box 261
Berrien Springs MI 49103
Phone: (269) 471-1202
Website: *berrienhistory.org*

Email: *info@berrienhistory.org*
Facebook: *@berrienhistory.org*

Tecumseh Historical Society
302 E. Chicago Blvd., P.O. Box 26
Tecumseh, MI 49286
Phone: (517) 423-2374
Website: *https://historictecumseh.org*
Email: *historictecumseh@gmail.com*
Facebook: *@tahs49286*

White Pigeon, MI:
St. Joseph County Historical Society
34 N. Main St.
Three Rivers MI 49093
Phone: (269) 274-6003
Email: *sjchs34@gmail.com*
Facebook: *@sjchsmi*

Ypsilanti Historical Society
220 N. Huron Street
Ypsilanti, MI 48197
Phone: (734) 217-8236
Website: *https://ypsihistory.org*
Email: *YHS.Archives@gmail.com or YHS.Museum@gmail.com*
Facebook: *@ypsihistory*

Historical Society of Michigan
7435 Westshire Drive
Lansing MI 48917
Phone: (517) 324-1828
Website: hsmichigan.org
Email: hsm@hsmichigan.org or email through the website form
Facebook: @hsmichigan

(***Note:*** The Historical Society of Michigan does not maintain research archives, but does publish two magazines and holds an annual history conference.)

MISSOURI:

St. Louis, MO:
Missouri Historical Society
P.O. Box 775460
St. Louis, MO 63177
Phone: (314) 746-4599 (general questions) or (314) 746-4510 (archival collections)
Website: *https://mohistory.org/society*
Email: *info@mohistory.org*
Facebook: *@mohistorymuseum*

NEW JERSEY:

Bordentown Historical Society
302 Farnsworth Ave.
P.O. Box 182
Bordentown, NJ 08505
Phone: (609) 298-1740
Website: *https://bordentownhistory.org*
Email: *bordentownhistoricalsociety@gmail.com*
Facebook: *@BordentownHistoricalSociety*

Burlington, NJ:
Burlington County Historical Society
457 High St.
Burlington NJ 08016
Phone: (609) 386-4773
Website: *https://burlingtoncountyhistoricalsociety.org/*
Email: *burlcohistsoc@verizon.net*
Facebook: *@BurlCoHistSoc*

Elizabethtown [Elizabethport], NJ:
Historical Society of Elizabeth, New Jersey
1045 East Jersey Street Suite #101
Elizabeth NJ 07201
Phone: 908-581-7555
Website: *www.visithistoricalelizabethnj.org*
Email: *hsenj1046@gmail.com*
Twitter: *@histelizabethnj*

NEW YORK:

Buffalo, NY:
Buffalo and Erie County Historical Society
(rebranded as Buffalo Historical Museum)
Museum: 1 Museum Ct., Buffalo NY 14216
Resource Center: 459 Forest Ave. Buffalo NY
Phone: (716) 873-9644
Website: *www.bechs.org*
Email: *kreed@buffalohistory.org*
   Library@buffalohistory.org

Historic Erie Canal Facebook Group:
Facebook: *@groups/592524657969509*

OHIO:

Cincinnati Historical Society
1301 Western Ave.
Cincinnati OH 45203
Phone: (513) 287-7000
Website: *cincymuseum.org*
Facebook: *@cincymuseum*

Cincinnati History Library and Archives
Email: *Library@cincymuseum.org*

Cleveland, Ohio:
Western Reserve Historical Society
10825 East Blvd.
Cleveland OH 44106
Phone: (216) 721-5722
Website: *wrhs.org*
Email: *info@wrhs.org;* or Research library: *aksindelar@wrhs.org*

Conneaut, Ohio:
Ashtabula County Historical Society
P.O. Box 36
Jefferson OH 44047
Phone: (866) 533-3277; or Susan Hill, Pres: (440) 294-2351

Website: *ashtcohs.com*
Email: *ashtcohs@gmail.com*

Marietta, Ohio:
Washington County Historical Society
346 Muskingum Drive
Marietta OH 45750
Phone: (740) 373-1788
Website: *https://www.wchshistory.org/*
Email: *wchs.ohio@gmail.com*
Facebook: *@WashingtonCountyHistoricalSocietyOhio*

Historical Marietta Ohio
Website: *http://www.historicalmarietta.blogspot.com*
Facebook: *@HistoricalMariettaOhio*
Email: *oldmariettaohio@gmail.com*

Portsmouth, Ohio:
Scioto County Heritage Museum
P.O. Box 697
Portsmouth OH 45662
Phone: (740) 307-2789
Website: *http://sciotocountyheritagemuseum.com*
Email: (John McHenry, Pres)*: johnkmchenry58@hotmail.com*
Facebook: *@Scioto-County-Heritage-Museum-101475985291713*

Wellsville (OH) Historical Society and River Museum
1003 Riverside Ave.
Wellsville OH 43968
Phone: (330) 532-1008
Website: *https://wellsville-historical-society-inc.hub.biz/*
Facebook: *@WellsvilleHistoricalSociety*
(No email listed, but messaging available on Facebook)

PENNSYLVANIA:

Alexandria, PA:
See: Huntingdon County (PA) Historical Society, below.

Blair County (PA) Historical Society
3419 Oak Lane
Altoona PA 16602
Phone: (814) 942-3916
Website: *www.blairhistory.org*
Email: *info@blairhistory.org*
Facebook: *@BlairHistory*

Blair County (PA) Genealogical Society
Phone: (814) 696-3492
Website: *bcgslibrary.org*
Facebook: *@bcgslibrary*

Blairsville, PA:
Historical Society of the Blairsville Area
116 E. Campbell St.
Blairsville PA 15717
Phone: (724) 459-0580
Website: *BlairsvilleHistoric.com*
Email: *hsba@verizon.net*
Facebook: *@Historical-Society-of-the-Blairsville-Area-1611605475616419*

Bristol, PA:
Bristol Cultural & Historical Foundation
321 Cedar St.
Bristol PA 19007
Phone: (215) 781-9895
Website: *bristolhistory.org*
Email: *bchf@bristolhistory.org*
Facebook: *@Bristol-Cultural-and-Historical-Foundation-366888976677210*

Columbia, PA:
Columbia Historic Preservation Society
19-21 N. Second St.
P.O. Box 578
Columbia PA 17512
Phone: (717) 684-2894
Website: *www.columbiapahistory.com*
Email: *columbiahistory717@gmail.com*
Facebook: *@cColumbia-Historic-Preservation-Society-236107089521/*

Harrisburg, PA:
Historical Society of Dauphin County
219 S. Front St.
Harrisburg PA 17104
Phone: (717) 233-3462
Website: *http://dauphincountyhistory.org/*
Email: *office@dauphincountyhistory.org*
Facebook: *@DauphinCountyHistory*

Hollidaysburg, PA:
Historic Hollidaysburg, Inc.
516 Walnut St.
Hollidaysburg PA 16648
Phone: (814) 696-0313
Email: *historichollidaysburginc@gmail.com*
Facebook: *@HistoricHollidaysburgInc*

Huntingdon County (PA) Historical Society (and Hartslog Heritage Museum)
P.O. Box 305
(Research Library: 106 - 4th St)
Huntingdon PA 16652
Phone: (814) 643-5449 (*leave message*)
Website: *www.huntingdonhistory.org*
Email: *hchsmail@gmail.com*
Facebook: *@Huntingdon-County-Historical-Society-291433218868*

Johnstown, PA:
Johnstown Area Heritage Association
201 Sixth Ave., P.O. Box 1889
Johnstown PA 15906 (15907 forP.O. Box)
Phone: (814) 539-1889, ext. 314 or 350
Website: *jaha.org*
Email: *aregan@jaha.org (Amy Regan, Historian) or sjohansson@jaha.org (Shelley Johansson, Director of Marketing & Communications)*
Facebook: *@theJAHA*

Juniata County (PA) Historical Society
498 Jefferson St. #B
Mifflintown PA 17059
Phone: (717) 436-5152

Website: *juniatacountyhistoricalsociety.org*
Email: *jchs1931@juniatacountyhistoricalsociety.org*
Facebook: *@JCHistory*

Lancaster, PA:
Lancaster History
230 N. President Ave.
Lancaster PA 17603
Phone: (717) 392-4633
Website: *www.lancasterhistory.org/*
Email: *info@lancasterhistory.org*
Facebook: *@lancasterhistory*

Lewistown, PA:
Mifflin County (PA) Historical Society
1 W. Market St.
Lewistown PA 17044
Phone: (717) 242-1022
Website: *MifflinCountyHistory.org*
Email: *office@MifflinCountyHistory.org*
Facebook: *@MifflinCountyHistoricalSociety*

Mexico, PA:
See: Juniata County (PA) Historical Society, above

Philadelphia, PA:
Historical Society of Philadelphia
1300 Locust St.
Philadelphia PA 19107
Phone: (215) 732-6200
Website: *https://www.portal.hsp.org/*
Email: *awilliams@hsp.org (Andrew Williams, Digital Services Archivist and Research Services Librarian) or chutto@hsp.org (Cary Hutto, Director of Archives)*
Facebook: *@historicalpa*

Pittsburgh, PA:
Detre Library and Archives, Sen. John Heinz History Center
1212 Smallman St.
Pittsburgh PA 15222
Phone: (412) 454-6364 (Library and Archives)
Website: *heinzhistorycenter.org*

Email: *Library@heinzhistorycenter.org*
Facebook: *@SenatorJohnHeinzHistoryCenter*

Saltsburg (PA) Historical Society
Rebecca B. Hadden Stone House Museum
105 Point Street
Saltsburg PA 15681
Phone: (724) 639-9003
Website: *http://RebeccaBHaddensHm.com*
Email: SaltsburgHistoricalSociety@yahoo.com
Facebook: @Saltsburg-Historical-Society

Waynesburg, PA: (later renamed McVeytown; see Mifflin County Historical Society, under Lewistown, above. *Note that the Waynesburg our traveler visited is not the same as today's Waynesburg in Greene County.*)

Williamsburg, PA:
See: Blair County (PA) Historical Society, above.

WEST VIRGINIA:

Guyandotte, WV: (now part of Huntington, WV):
Cabell-Wayne County Historical Society
P.O. Box 9412
Huntington WV 25704

Wayne Co. (WV) Genealogical and Historical Society:
P.O. Box 787
Wayne, WV 22570-0787
Website: *wcghs.com*
Email: *mail@wcghs.com*

Wheeling, WV:
Ohio County Public Library (Wheeling WV)
52 - 16th Street
Wheeling WV 26003
Phone: (304) 232-0244
Website: *http://www.ohiocountylibrary.org*
Email: *info@ohiocountylibrary.org*
Facebook: *@ohiocountylibrary*

www.ingramcontent.com/pod-product-compliance
Lightning Source LLC
Chambersburg PA
CBHW070808100426
42742CB00012B/2301